THE
STRESS
FACTOR

A GUIDE TO MORE RELAXED LIVING

H.E. STANTON

An OPTIMA book

© H.E. Stanton 1983

First published in Australia in 1983 by
Fontana Books, Sydney

This edition published in Great Britain in 1988 by
Macdonald Optima, a division of
Macdonald & Co. (Publishers) Ltd

A member of Maxwell Pergamon Publishing Corporation plc

British Library Cataloguing in Publication Data
Stanton, H.E. (Harry E.)
    The stress factor.
    1. Man. Stress. Self-treatment
    I. Title
    158.1

    ISBN 0-356-15192-1

Macdonald & Co. (Publishers) Ltd
3rd Floor
Greater London House
Hampstead Road
London NW1 7QX

Printed and bound in Great Britain at
The Guernsey Press

Dedication

To Valerie, Peter and Lynda who have helped me
transform distress into eustress

Acknowledgements

In the text I have acknowledged my debt to workers in the area of stress such as the late Hans Selye. I should also like to express my appreciation to my family, my patients, my students, and my colleagues from whom I have learned much. It is through observing how others have experienced and coped with stress that I have been able to live my own life more comfortably. Special thanks is due to Sylvia Murrell for her good-humoured assistance in the typing of the manuscript.

Contents

1 Introduction

Health and wellness

Although it might appear that health in Western countries has improved dramatically during the twentieth century, it also appears that there has been an equally dramatic decline in 'wellness'. A contradiction in terms? Not really. Many infectious diseases, such as tuberculosis and diphtheria, have been virtually eliminated, yet stress-related illnesses, such as heart attacks, hardening of the arteries and cirrhosis of the liver, are increasing.

Perhaps the apparent contradiction is a function of the medical definition of health as the absence of any substantial symptoms indicating an underlying disease process. If this definition is adopted, a person could experience severe headaches, indigestion, insomnia, constipation and fatigue, though perhaps not all at the same time, and be pronounced healthy by a doctor. This person would be classified as healthy, yet from his or her own viewpoint, he or she would not feel well. Somewhat cynically, Carlton Fredericks, the prominent American nutritionist, has commented that: 'The typical doctor's definition of good health is the ability to remain upright in a strong wind.'

The medical definition of health given above suggests that some doctors have overlooked the main reason for most illness—our own emotions and behaviour. Although estimates vary considerably, it would seem reasonable to assert that approximately three-quarters of patients found in doctors' waiting rooms have emotionally induced disorders. These people are usually treated by tranquillizers, a procedure which leaves untouched the cause of their problem, namely the way of life they choose to adopt.

As I have pointed out in my earlier book, *The Healing Factor: A Guide to Positive Health*, the key principle underlying the concept of wellness is *personal responsibility*. To attain the feeling of being fit and healthy there are many things we can do for ourselves. These include the use of healing systems such as homeo-pathy, Bach flower remedies, Schussler biochemic cell salts and reflexology, as well as the adoption of a healthy lifestyle through good nutrition, weight control, exercise and improved breathing.

Our health, or feeling of wellness, is to a great extent a product of what we do with our body and with our thoughts. Overeating, smoking, drug abuse, and over-indulgence in alcohol are choices we can make or unmake. Similarly, we can choose to think in positive ways which are productive of well-being or indulge in negative thinking, guilt, blame and fear which under-mine our physical and mental health.

What is mental health?

According to the staff of the famous United States Menninger Foundation, being mentally healthy involves behaving consistently. Firstly, it is important to have a *wide variety of sources of gratification*. People who are mentally healthy find pleasure in many different ways and from many different things. Should one source of gratification be removed, perhaps through moving to another State and losing contact with friends, they have alternatives, such as hobbies, sport or work, which fill the gap until new friends are made.

A second mode of behaviour characteristic of mentally healthy people is their *recognition and acceptance of their strengths and weaknesses*. They are reasonably accurate in their self-assessment, in the picture of themselves which they hold. Also, they are comfortable with themselves, in marked contrast to the self-hating individual who transfers his negative opinion of himself to virtually everyone with whom he comes into contact. Avoiding false modesty, mentally healthy people do not belittle their talents and skills. However, neither do they try to conceal their weaknesses from themselves. Such people can accept themselves as they are without striving to be someone else. Similarly, they are able to accept others as individuals who have every right to be different from themselves.

Thirdly, mentally healthy people are *active and productive*, using their resources to serve their own needs and those of other people. Though they enjoy using the skills they possess, there is no feeling of being driven, of having to produce in order to prove themselves worthwhile.

Possession of this attitude, of accepting that human beings are important in themselves quite apart from what they may do, enables such people to be in control of their activities. They do not permit their activities to take charge of them, nor do they worry about what they cannot do. As Edward Everett Hale has put it:

> I am only one, but I am one.
> I cannot do everything, but I can do something.
> And I will not let what I cannot do
> Interfere with what I can do.

Finally, mentally healthy people tend to be *flexible under stress*. When faced with problems, they are able to see alternative solutions rather than being rigidly stuck with one way of looking at things. Stress, as will become apparent in the next chapter, is not something lurking 'out there' waiting to pounce on us. Rather, it is largely a matter of how much threat or danger a person sees in his or her environment. Therefore, the more flexible individual who has a wide variety of solutions to problems is likely to perceive less threat because he or she feels reasonably confident of finding answers to the demands of everyday life.

Sufferers from stress and their support systems

Sufferers from stress do not necessarily display a defined set of symptoms, for the human body responds in many ways to the demands placed upon it. In some cases, it is primarily physical symptoms such as headaches or indigestion which people display in response to excessive amounts of stress, whereas in others mental states such as anxiety and depression are noticeable.

We often attempt to compare the effects of one source of disease with another in terms of numbers of deaths. However, we cannot really ascertain how many people have died due to the effects of prolonged stress as opposed to the effects of poor diet, excessive smoking, over-indulgence in alcohol or lack of exercise. These factors are all inter-related, though medical evidence now leaves little doubt that strain derived from work and personal problems does play an important part in heart attacks. In Western countries the numbers of deaths due to heart diseases continue to rise each year, as does the number of fatal strokes suffered by men in their fifties, and it appears that the role of stress in this state of affairs is assuming an ever increasing importance.

So far-reaching are the effects of stress on the mind and body that they tend to exacerbate many diseases. Tension, strain, and anxiety often produce harmful physiological changes in the body which render it less effective in coping with the problems of the environment. Although there may be no direct link between stress and a specific disease, because the mind and body operate as a whole any adverse changes in, say, the cardiovascular system must inevitably have an effect on the body's capability for dealing with disorders which cannot themselves be blamed on exposure to stress or strain.

To put it simply, then, stress exerts a very pervasive influence over our health, both physical and mental. We therefore seek support systems to help us cope more successfully. The most popular of these are alcohol, tobacco and tranquillizers. It is an interesting quirk of human nature that we see our own particular 'crutch' as permissible, but those of others as true vices. I well remember a magistrate castigating a young man who appeared before him on a marijuana smoking charge, condemning him for his anti-social behaviour. The magistrate himself was verging on alcoholism but obviously saw his drug as different and somehow 'better'.

Most of us seem to need something to help us handle the stresses of our lives. As American psychologist Vernon Coleman has expressed it in *Stress Control*: ' . . . the human organism seems doomed to dependence on something. Whether that something is tobacco, alcohol, Valium or gambling it is an essential part of life. The human organism, it seems, is unable to survive without some form of artificial crutch.'

This is not just a modern phenomenum. Long before the pressures of modern living were documented as fully as they now are, methods of support were available to those people unable to cope without them. Drugs such as alcohol and opium were probably the most common of these, but religion in its various forms has also provided support for millions of people—Karl Marx, for example, described it as the 'opium of the people'. Today, for many people, television has become the main support system, providing as it does company, excitement and relaxation.

Assuming then, that most of us need some form of

'crutch', it seems rather counter-productive to deliberately seek one which is particularly damaging. Yet, as Coleman says, who can ascertain where most harm lies, for, 'Alcohol destroys the liver, tobacco ruins the lungs, television affects the mind, gambling results in ruin and poverty. The non-prescribed drugs have well-publicized dangers as do the prescribed drugs. Even religion has its dangers.' On the other hand, many would see it as one of the more beneficent 'crutches'.

This book and its role

Since each of us is personally biased towards one or another of these 'crutches' we find it extremely difficult to decide on the least harmful form of support to adopt. I cannot tell you what decision to make. However, by discussing alternative ways of handling stress, I may be able to help you reduce your dependence on a 'crutch' about which you are uneasy. As will become obvious in the pages which follow, I believe that we can handle our lives reasonably successfully by exercising more control over our thought processes, by using exercise to channel off tension, by relaxing, and by using harmless natural substances which exert a calming effect. The approach I suggest does not appear likely to harm anybody. On the contrary, it would seem to engender many beneficial effects quite at variance with the damage of the support systems mentioned earlier in this chapter.

It is usually helpful to have another viewpoint, one which may provide an alternative to the way you are at present managing your life and its attendant stresses. Most of the issues which confront you each day do not require you to gain deep insights into your own personality before you can successfully resolve them. Rather, through exposure to another viewpoint, you may gain a different perspective which enables you to tackle the issue anew with a greater hope of success, as you pursue new angles, new avenues for further effort.

No one can tell another person how to live his or her life. I have no desire to do so myself. Nor do I wish to simply load you with more information. We have been conditioned all our lives to believe that knowledge by itself is very helpful—so we acquire more and more knowledge and rarely translate it into habits of action. That is, we are educated to be coaches rather than players, critics rather than creators. Talking, and sometimes thinking, have replaced doing, so that what we learn is more decorative than functional. If we have a problem we are urged to gain 'insight' into it, perhaps through visiting a psychiatrist once or twice a week for four or five years. We learn to talk intelligently about our problem, gaining a great deal of knowledge about it—but we still have it.

So our difficulty is that we are more observers of our own lives than performers. Knowing that something is true does not make it valuable: we have to *use* this knowledge. Then we can change our lives. This is what I hope you will be able to do with the ideas set out in this book. *Use them.* Find out which ones work for you and enhance your life as your learn to control stress more effectively. Reading a self-help book can be very beneficial if you are willing to try new things and allow the suggestions given to stimulate you to experiment with your own behaviour. On the other hand, reading a book such as this can be a waste of time if all you do is analyse the ideas presented, without finding out if they might actually work for you. By acting in such a way, you promise yourself a change intellectually, but never take the first positive steps.

The ideas for managing stress outlined in this book *do* work—not necessarily for every person every time, but for most people most of the time. They are not perfect . . . so do not set yourself up for disappointment by insisting that every idea you try must always be one hundred per cent successful. It is rare in life to find such an occurrence. In fact, it is likely to be more helpful to adopt a philosophy such as Hugh Prather's, when he writes in *I Touch the Earth, the Earth Touches Me:*

> By approaching my problems with 'What might make things a little better?' rather than 'What is the solution?' I avoid setting myself up for certain frustration. My experience has shown me that I am not going to solve anything in one stroke, at best I am only going to chip away at it.

Prather, too, has pointed out that nothing is exactly the way he would like it to be—because that is simply the way life is. Acceptance of this means that there is one battle he does not have to fight any more. If you, too, can settle for something less than a perfect solution to your problems with handling stress, you are likely to derive a great deal of value from this book. Adoption of the ideas contained within its pages will certainly 'make things a little better' and, quite likely, make them a lot better.

This is what has happened for the people whom I have used as examples and 'case studies'. Although I have changed their names to avoid causing them any embarrassment, they are quite real and their experiences have been those I describe in the following chapters.

2 Understanding Stress

Indications of stress

John Kiel, normally a reasonably easy-going, even-tempered man, raged at his wife for being late with his evening meal. Later, he became extremely irritable because technical faults were interrupting a television programme he was watching. During ensuing weeks, John's restlessness increased markedly and he found it difficult to relax. Although his usual pattern was one of allowing problems to take care of themselves, he became more worried about things, particularly past events which, he realized, would not be changed one iota by his fretting. John's concentration at work suffered, too, as he found it quite difficult to focus his mind upon the job at hand. As a result, he was making far more mistakes and errors of judgement than he had done previously.

An observer might describe John as being under stress. He could well use the same label for Maureen Shiels. A housewife and mother of two young children, she complained of a wide variety of physical symptoms. Most days she suffered from chest pains, diarrhoea, headaches, indigestion, insomnia, heart palpitations and tiredness. Though all these symptoms would not necessarily appear every day, they were present much of the time. In addition, Maureen exhibited somewhat the same mental symptoms as John. She found it difficult to relax properly, the noise created by her children playing became intolerable, and she would over-react to trivial disturbances with short-tempered irritability. Her memory and concentration were not good and she was subject to fits of uncontrolled emotion resulting in frequent episodes of crying.

Barry Ferguson's stress was initially a function of his job as foreman in a shoe factory, but inevitably spilled over into his home life. Because of dissatisfaction with his work, he became increasingly inefficient and fatigued, waking up feeling tired and continuing feeling tired throughout the day. 'Escape activities' increased as Barry ate, smoked and drank more. These signals of stress he passed off as simply being part of modern life, but he became more concerned as he developed backaches, headaches, a possible ulcer and frequent skin irritations, together with feelings of anger and depression.

John, Maureen and Barry are people under stress. How do we know? What causes us to label them in this way?

Although people exhibit a variety of stress symptoms, there are certain indicators which are usually present. In John's case, he displayed the four leading signs of emotional stress. Specifically he was

- irritable and angry if things did not go as he wished
- restless and unable to relax
- worrying about things which worrying would not help
- having difficulty in concentrating.

In addition, his ability to tolerate ambiguity and to sort out the trivial from the important had lessened so that he was making more and more mistakes.

Maureen had these early warning mental signs of stress together with impaired memory and uncontrolled emotional outbursts. She also revealed a number of physical symptoms often linked to stress. Most people have a weak point in their systems and it is here that the first symptoms usually appear. Some may suffer from indigestion when worried or anxious; others develop throat trouble or headaches. However, as the pressure increases, a multitude of additional physical ailments follow in the wake of these early warning signs.

Inefficiency in a job he disliked was Barry's most obvious sign of stress, but he shared many of John's and Maureen's symptoms, too. These were manifested on three levels:

- The *psychological*, with anxiety and irritability being the first important signs that an individual feels unable to cope with his or her environment. Concentrating and thinking become difficult, emphasis falling on short-term rather than long-term outcomes.

- The *physical*, where the preoccupation with problems and the inability to relax produce headaches, stomach upsets and sleeping problems. If nothing is done to relieve stress, then high blood pressure and ulcers often occur.

- The *behavioural*, where people smoke more and drink more alcohol, use tranquilizers and withdraw from relationships which are proving difficult. Symptoms such as hair twirling, nail biting, ankle tapping, clenching fists and furrowing of the brow are quite common.

These indicators can help us judge if we are running above or below the stress level that suits us best. Through self-awareness we can develop an instinctive feeling which guides us, for stress is the body's non-specific response to *any* demand placed on it, whether pleasant or unpleasant. Sitting in the dentist's chair is stressful. So, too, is sharing a passionate embrace with a lover. In both cases our reaction is the same: quickened breathing, an increased pulse rate, and many other interesting changes which will be elaborated later in this chapter.

Stress is not, then, all bad—and our aim should not be to avoid it completely. Not only would this be impossible—it would also be undesirable, for we would miss many of life's 'highs'. Rather, we might better aim at recognizing our typical response to stress and modulate our lives so that we can keep ourselves, for at least much of the time, at an optimum level of arousal. Before we can modulate our lives in this way, we need to answer the question: 'What is stress?'

What is stress?

When people are asked about the stress they feel, they usually have a clear idea of what they are talking about. Physiological and psychological symptoms such as those described earlier in this chapter are mentioned frequently, as are feelings of being unable to cope, lack of control of situations and of oneself, and a general sense of unease. These discomforting symptoms indicate that we are doing something injurious to ourselves, and we can become easily demoralized. That is, we feel unable to deal with demands made upon us by our environment while, at the same time, realizing we have to do so. Anxiety is the usual result of this conflict, together with resentment and frustration which become apparent when there are either too many or too few demands made upon us.

In common language, the label 'stress' is associated with distress, meaning any kind of demand, burden, pressure or hardship. When people talk about 'the stress of modern living', they mean, usually, those circumstances which generate worry, tension and frustration. I have an acquaintance who frequently talks in this way, displaying a sort of pride that he is living in an era which is experiencing so much stress.

Yet every era has been an age of anxiety. Years ago the threat of nuclear warfare and worldwide pollution did not hang over our heads, but there existed the devastation of plague, other highly dangerous and infectious diseases, the misery of economic depression, and the fear of flood, fire and famine. Everything in human life is uncertain. Today you may be rich, tomorrow poor.

Biologically speaking, stress means anything constituting a threat, either real or imagined, which would damage the organism. Hans Selye, the world's foremost researcher into stress, defines it as 'the rate of wear and tear on the body', and has demonstrated that there is a generalized adaptive response whether the agent we face is pleasant or unpleasant. Cold, heat, rage, happiness, drugs, boredom, excitement, pain, hormones, grief and joy all elicit the stress reactions of the body in the same way. This response we will look at more carefully in the next section of this chapter.

Since it is difficult to define stress precisely, it is becoming common to speak of 'arousal' instead. This term 'arousal' covers the idea of 'stirring up' and does describe rather well how the body prepares itself for action when some threat is perceived. As I mentioned earlier, it is desirable for us to observe how we react to stress and attempt to keep ourselves at our optimum level of arousal.

Unfortunately, though psychologists have pointed out that under-arousal and over-arousal both impair performance, they have not been very helpful in pointing out how we find our most appropriate level of being 'stirred-up'. If we are under-stimulated, we are too relaxed to achieve well; if we are over-stimulated, our anxiety interferes with whatever we are trying to do. In his book *Executive Health*, Andrew Melhuish illustrates this problem graphically (*see next page*).

So we can talk of stress in terms of the extent to which we are aroused by our environment, either pleasantly or unpleasantly. Another way of looking at it is in terms of our *confidence level*. Pressure or demands that we can handle increase our confidence. Through responding to the challenge we experience the pleasant aspect of stress.

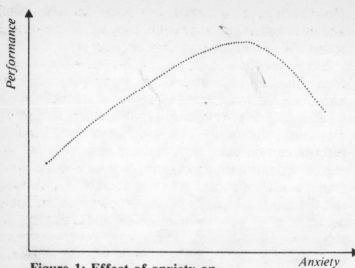

Figure 1: Effect of anxiety on performance: Yerkes-Dobson Law

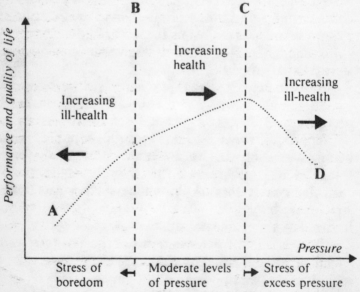

Figure 2: Medical extension of Yerkes-Dobson Law

However, in a situation where we experience frustration and even panic at not achieving a goal, our confidence wanes. We feel undue anxiety and strain.

Bill Rogers felt this anxiety on his retirement from the firm where he had worked for many years. His work had given him his status. It was the prop which gave him a sense of self-esteem and importance. Now this prop was gone. Bill felt he had worked most of his life to reach a certain goal, a position of responsibility as an executive, and now he was told that he was useless. He found it difficult to adapt to the loss of status and his self-confidence just seemed to ebb away. What use was he to anyone? The more he worried about his non-status, non-important role as a retired person, the more his anxiety level rose and the greater pressure of stress he felt. Unless Bill adopts a different viewpoint on what is meaningful in his life, he is likely to die very quickly. Things are worth what we make them worth, and Bill is creating tremendous stress for himself by choosing to think of his work as the entire reason for his existence. Many women make the same mistake by feeling their life is ended because their children, the prime reason for their existence, have left home.

Bill will have to adjust to changed circumstances, as will the woman whose children have left home. Stress is a matter of demands. Anything that places an extra demand on you creates stress and this requires adjustment on your part. Bill, in order to survive, will need to choose to think differently, to see that there are things he can do in his retirement, such as new hobbies, recreations, sports, which will give him a sense of confidence in his own abilities. As he does so, so the self-created stress eases. By setting new goals, new challenges, Bill can turn his *distress* into *eustress*.

Eustress and distress

Eustress, according to the world's foremost researcher in the field, the late Hans Selye, is the stress of achievement, triumph and exhilaration. It is the stress of winning and, as such, we welcome it for the positive feelings it brings. Distress, on the other hand, is the stress of losing, when we feel insecure, inadequate, helpless, despairing and disappointed. Most people concern themselves with this darker aspect. In fact, when people talk of stress they usually mean Selye's distress. Because of this common meaning, when I talk of ways of managing stress, I will use the term in this negative way. After all, we do not have to find ways of managing eustress, for the keyed-up feeling of winning is reward in itself and can be enjoyed to the full.

It is understandable that stress is usually seen as distress, for it is always present. The jangling telephone, the interminable traffic jam, the never-ending decisions to be made while shopping, the strain of examinations, and of separation and illness, are part of the fabric of life. So too, of course, is eustress, with the athlete keyed-up to compete, the entertainer giving a great performance, and the man or woman solving a difficult problem. Any physical effort requires us to be aroused to some degree or another and it is through the stretching influence of stress that people and entire communities find unexpected resources within themselves which enable them to meet new challenges.

It is interesting to note that, just as we usually equate stress with distress, we also tend to equate it with an overload of demands placed upon us. We are asked to do too much, there is too much pressure, and we become anxious and frustrated. Yet people cannot tolerate underload either. Too *little* of the external stimuli considered stressful often produces symptoms similar to those produced by overload. A number of sensory deprivation experiments have confirmed this phenemonon. Men and women have been suspended underwater in a womb-like tank in an unchanging environment where they could see, hear and feel nothing. None has been able to tolerate such conditions for more than six hours presumably because they had nothing to stimulate them in the unvarying environment to which they were exposed.

Thus, it appears our nervous system needs constant stimulation to function effectively. When the arousal or stress level falls too low, people seek excitement in work and play; when it rises too high, people can dissipate it by exercise, meditation, or any of the other methods outlined in the chapters on managing stress. So, the way we achieve an optimum level of arousal is to turn up underloads and turn down overloads.

When stress is handled effectively it provides the motivation which encourages us to overcome the obstacles blocking us from the achievement of our hopes and goals. This is *eustress*. When it is allowed to get out of control, it leads to illness, poor performance, and even death. This is *distress*. However, stress need not become distress if its symptoms are seen as providing an early warning system making us aware of situations which threaten our well-being.

The deliberate stress-seeker is in a somewhat different position from the individual who heeds the warning signs and avoids further stressful situations. Such a person is already too aroused and realizes that further arousal will turn his stress into distress. However, the mountain climber, racing car driver, sky diver and even the business executive often deliberately seek to become immersed in stress-provoking situations. They do so because of the euphoric feelings of being intensely alive, of living dangerously. By pitting themselves against difficult or even threatening situations they increase an arousal level that is probably initially quite low, to that optimum level where they perform at their best.

Though overcoming challenges is a stimulus which can bring a marvellous 'high', we do seem to have within us a defence mechanism against too much challenge. When our arousal level is too high we become ill, or develop pain as a respectable way of opting out of a difficult situation. In the Victorian era, people got the 'vapours' when life became uncongenial. Today we become 'stressed', but the mechanism is the same, for we are reacting to a situation whose demands we cannot meet. Our stress reaction, which is usually pain in one form or another, allows us to retire temporarily from the situation. It is also a sign that we need to take a break. If we do not heed such a sign, we are likely to become increasingly distressed. Obviously, then, our stress reaction or response merits closer examination.

The stress response

As I have mentioned earlier, Selye has demonstrated that the human body responds in the same way to everything, be it a 'flu virus, cold temperatures, a car accident or emotions such as fear and anger. In the pre-Selye era, scientists believed there was a different physical reaction to each one of these agents. What, then, is this stress response which occurs whenever we are faced with any demand from our environment?

Imagine Og, a caveman who may well be one of your ancestors. As he is hunting for food in the prehistoric jungle, he comes face to face with a dinosaur. As soon as Og recognizes his danger, which happens virtually immediately, his muscles tense for action, a reflex response by-passing the brain. Thus he is prepared to fight or run away. The message of danger is then received by the brain which initiates dramatic changes by means of the hypothalamus. This centre integrates all body functions which are not normally under our conscious control.

Og's hypothalamus releases chemicals which quickly reach the pituitary gland hanging on a short stem just below it. Stimulated by these chemicals, the pituitary provides hormones which are carried by the blood to the adrenal glands located on top of the kidneys. In turn, the adrenals pump out adrenalin and epinephrine hormones which create drastic changes in Og's system, every part of the body being involved. His heart beats faster and blood pressure rises. His digestion is interrupted as blood flows to the muscles. The salivary glands dry up, the stomach and intestines stop working, and the sphincter muscles close to avoid defaecation and urination taking place.

Because the lungs must take in more air to provide oxygen and get rid of more carbon dioxide, Og's breathing becomes deeper and faster. His skin changes, too. As he is likely to become overheated in vigorous activity, Og starts sweating, a process designed to cool his body. So that blood may be diverted to the muscles that urgently need it at this time, Og's capillary blood vessels constrict—he looks quite pale. Further energy is provided to his muscles through an increase in blood sugar stimulated by other hormones called gluco-corticoids.

All these changes take place incredibly rapidly. Og's 'fight or flight' response has readied him to take immediate action. The chemicals flooding his system will be used through vigorous use of his muscles. Once he has either overcome the dinosaur or successfully run away and eluded it, his body calms down. His pancreas will produce more insulin to bring the blood sugar down to normal; his heart rate slows down with an attendant drop in blood pressure; in his liver, hormones will be neutralized; his digestion will be resumed and the lactic acid created through muscular exertion neutralized.

This process of responding to stress with the 'fight or flight' reaction and then using up the chemicals involved in muscular activity seems admirably suited to the way our primitive ancestors lived. It does not seem to be so appropriate in the circumstances of modern living whereby our stress response is easily triggered by different sorts of demands which do not give us the opportunity to burn up the hormones flooding our system or release pent-up energy and fear. As a result, many people feel tense much of the time, somewhat like cars that are constantly revved up but which never actually move.

The great enemy of human health is not danger, emotional upheaval or the occasional crisis. Rather, it is the prolonged unrelieved state of worry, anxiety and arousal. The stress response mobilizes the body to cope with short-term crises and it does this admirably. Usually, the 'fight or flight' process enables us to solve the immediate problem quickly, sometimes in a matter of minutes and certainly within several hours, and then allows our bodies to return to their normal level of lower activation.

However, the stress response is far less suited to handling the stress of modern city living. The effects of crowding, traffic, noise, verbal battles with the boss, co-workers and the family, violent, unsettling television programmes, and anxiety-provoking news reports serve to maintain, in many people, a continuous, unrelieved state of high arousal for a large part of their day. This is chronic stress. It often results in a serious breakdown of health.

When our stress reaction is triggered too often and too intensely, our bodies tends to accumulate the effects of the chemicals which ready us for action. Although the whole body suffers, it is usually our weakest link which breaks down first. This may be physical, as it is when we come down with one bad cold after another. It could be mental as we slide into a state of misery and depression. It could also be sexual. A prolonged stress reaction sharply decreases the level of the primary male hormone, testosterone, which exerts a direct influence on the sex drive. The result is a man who progressively loses interest in sex, possibly experiences impotence, worries about this, and further increases his stress level by so doing. Women, too, experience a reduction of an important sex hormone, progesterone, during prolonged stress. Frigidity can be the result.

Perhaps the stress response has become obsolete. For millions of years, the struggle against stress has depended on the success of a single strategy—reduce arousal by fight or flight. Yet we now live in a different world from the one in which this strategy was first developed. Machines have replaced muscle power, work has become highly specialized, and work stress goes unrelieved. In most jobs, the fight and flight reaction is ineffective because the stress continues day after day, week after week, with nothing to provide the necessary interruption to allow restoration. Perhaps *nothing* is too strong a word, for there are tea breaks, weekends off the job and holidays. These do provide the necessary interruption as long as they are used in a stress-relieving way. Often they are not.

If during tea breaks we drink caffeine, we raise our arousal level. This effect is compounded by smoking, for nicotine is a stimulant. At weekends, a quiet round of golf may raise the blood pressure far higher than any work stress will do, and social activities with noise and pressure may not serve well to provide relaxation. If holidays are a rush from one place to another, full of frantic activity, they too are unlikely to help the work-stressed individual very much, although vigorous muscular activity is likely to be useful in reducing the accumulation of stress chemicals in the body. This point will be elaborated in the chapters dealing with managing stress.

The 'fight or flight' response is very important for all animals when life is threatened, but human beings differ in that we can produce these physical and chemical changes for situations that do not require vigorous muscular activity. Car drivers fuming in a traffic jam, parents exasperated by their children's questions, executives frustrated by a meeting which is getting nowhere, employees arguing with their bosses—all are likely to produce the same response as someone whose life is threatened. To illustrate: someone doing addition at the rate of 40 one-digit numbers per minute more than doubles his or her adrenalin output, while an interpreter doing simultaneous interpretation is likely to record a pulse rate of up to 160 beats a minute. These people react as if they were engaged in battle instead of sitting still in a chair.

Further, the human brain is sufficiently developed for us to dwell on past events or imagine future ones. Thus, instead of our reactions to stress being short-lived, they can persist over long periods. Such persistent emotional states can be profoundly damaging to the body.

Hans Selye has talked about this problem in terms of the *general adaptation syndrome*. Whenever a demand is made upon us, we engage in a detailed sequence of behaviour:

- There is an initial alarm reaction of surprise and anxiety, perhaps because of our inexperience in dealing with a new situation. This is the fight-and-flight response already described.
- A stage of resistance follows during which we may learn to cope effectively with the demand. If so, our body functions return to normal after we have done so.
- If not, there is a final stage of exhaustion, a depletion of energy reserves which leads to fatigue. This occurs if severe stress continues unabated. The symptoms of the alarm or fight-and-flight reaction continue over such a long period that they cannot be reversed. When this happens, according to Selye, the animal dies because its fund of 'adaptive energy' is exhausted. It is unable to alter its behaviour in order to accommodate the incessant stress.

It seems that modern man has replaced intermittent intense stress, which was a natural part of living, with man-made stresses which are more or less constant. It is this constant low-level arousal which pushes us into the second state of resistance, and finally, the third stage of exhaustion and disease. Our highly developed brain finds pleasant or unpleasant connotations in a vast number of situations and events. Not only do we react to tangible, physical stresses like heat, cold and injury, but also to many symbolic or imagined threats or pleasures. The objective nature of these is not nearly as important as their meaning to a particular individual at a particular moment.

Our attitude to pain, for example, depends more on the meaning attached to it than on its severity. Soldiers wounded in action often feel little pain when hospitalized after operations, perhaps due to their relief at escaping from the battlefield. By contrast, civilians frequently complain of severe post-operative pain after quite minor surgery. Perhaps stressors, then, are relatively neutral and the way we perceive them is what gives them their power.

The perception of stress

It is easy to think of our environment as being full of stressors, things ready to create stress for us. But is this really true? It seems more reasonable to argue that it is *our reactions* to stressors which cause most of our problems. That is, we create our own stress by the choices we make. You are walking through the city and notice that a couple of people give you a second look. Now you don't know why they are looking at you, and you have a choice about how you want to think about this. Probably most people think, 'What is wrong with me?' They check on their clothes, find nothing out of place, but continue worrying. Thus they create stress for themselves. Yet you could think, 'I must look good today.' This thought generates no stress, just a pleasant feeling. You might be wrong, of course. People may not be looking at you because you are looking good. However, as long as you do not know the reason for their behaviour, I believe it is preferable to choose to think in a way that is non-stressful than in a way that produces stress.

It is a matter of how you perceive information. You wake sluggishly, look at the clock, and see the time is 8.55 a.m. If it is a weekday, and you are due at work by 9.00 a.m., the time shown by your clock is a negative stressor. That is, it makes you anxious. However, if it is Sunday, and you can anticipate a lazy day with no pressing commitments, the clock generates no anxiety or stress. The information provided is the same in both cases. It is the way you perceive this information that determines how you will respond.

One man's stress is another man's stimulus, and it is often very difficult to predict how an individual will react to apparently stressful change. At one time, all anxiety and tension were labelled as abnormal. We now accept that a moderate amount of stress is healthy and stimulating. The person who works long hours at a high powered job is still thought of as being highly stressed. Not necessarily so. Many surveys have found that people often thrive in such situations and that it is the individual with the routine, ordinary job, such as production line work or housework, who is the one more likely to develop heart disease and ulcers caused by stress overload.

It seems that stress resides neither in the situation nor in the person. Rather, it depends on an interaction between the two, with stress arising from the way a person appraises an event and adapts to it. In his book *Stress without Distress*, Selye has put it this way:

> Most people who want to accomplish something are ambitious and live in stress. They need it . . . stress is not something to be avoided, rather it is the spice of life. The only way to be free of all stress would be to do nothing at all. Complete freedom from stress is death because all human activity involves stress.

Obviously, then, the common assumption that stress is a bad thing which should be avoided is not particularly accurate. A more helpful way of looking at it is in terms of the arousal idea explained earlier. If stress is largely a function of how we choose to react to the events in our environment, we do have considerable power to adopt an attitude which will keep us operating at an optimum level of arousal.

Each of us 'converts' events into stress in our own way. Different people react quite differently to the same pressure situation. Judith Denmare was asked to give a short talk on her recent overseas trip to a large audience of women. She was paralysed by fear as the time approached for her to stand up and speak. For Judy, the neutral event of giving a talk had become a negative stressor which imposed great strain upon her. She had 'converted' the event into distress by the way she chose to think about it. 'All those people. I'm so inadequate. They wouldn't be interested in what I have to say. They'll make me look foolish by asking awkward questions.' No one makes Judy think this way. She chooses to do so—and puts herself under tremendous pressure.

Jane Henderson spoke to the same women's group several weeks later. She saw the 'demand' as a challenge, a chance to demonstrate she could handle the situation. She chose to think of the audience as being on her side, as wanting to help her, and of herself as having something interesting to say. Jane's level of arousal was high, as was Judy's, but she experienced the eustress of challenge, not the distress Judy experienced. The same event was perceived very differently by the two women concerned.

Our personal history of experience and learned reactions influences how we handle demands from the environment, for the ability to handle pressure varies among people and is something of a learned skill. Highly reactive people, such as Judy, seem to meet even the most minor of disturbances as if they were crises. They react just as strongly to minor frustrations, such as dropping a cup and breaking it, as to fairly major provocations such as a child's illness. Everything is horrible, awful, and catastrophic.

On the other hand, people like Jane have learned less highly reactive ways of dealing with environmental demands. They seem to reserve the panic behaviour, if they ever do really panic at all, for situations that are crises. That is, Jane would usually be able to regulate the intensity of her reaction to the relative seriousness of the situation.

Like beauty, stress lies in the eye of the beholder. If you perceive threat in a situation, it is stressful; if you perceive no threat in a situation, it is not stressful. Some of us, unfortunately, see threat everywhere and are in a constant state of tension. Others see little threat around them and are relatively relaxed. Such differing ways of regarding the world are often a function of self-esteem. The confident person, such as Jane, welcomes a challenge, whereas Judy, a person with low self-esteem, sees danger and personal threat.

People, then, have differing responses to seemingly similar stress situations. Also, any one individual is likely to have varying abilities to deal with different types of demand or challenge. An acquaintance of mine, Bob Handley, loves business meetings. This is a source of some amazement to me as I dislike such gatherings. However, Bob sees them as a welcome break in his routine, an opportunity to interact with other people in a way he enjoys. Under these circumstances, he is relaxed, affable and at ease, presenting information clearly and effectively. No distress there. Yet, when Bob has to do anything with his hands such as replacing a fuse or hammering a nail, he is tense, irritable, frustrated. Things always go wrong. He suffers distress. So, although some people react with distress to virtually every environmental demand, others, like Bob, do so only to some events. Other events pose no threat at all.

Gail Harvey and her husband, Dennis, run an antique business. Gail is, by far, the more adventurous in her buying, willing to take risks in backing her judgement. Dennis is ultra-conservative and often becomes almost panic stricken at some of his wife's buys. Yet on a recent holiday trip, while riding a jet-boat in a swiftly flowing river, Dennis felt exhilarated and Gail was in a state of panic and terror.

Perhaps the most widely documented aspect of how different types of people react differently to stress is the Friedman and Rosenman concept of Type A and Type B personalities. In their book, *Type A Behaviour and Your Heart*, they point out that people with certain personality characteristics subject themselves to tremendous pressure and by so doing increase their chances of having a heart attack. These *Type A people*, or 'hostile achievers' as they have also been called, tend to:
- set themselves harsh deadlines and quotas
- be heavily achievement oriented
- push themselves and others to capacity
- react to frustration with hostility
- always appear pressed for time
- be highly competitive in everything they do.

By contrast, *Type B people* tend to:
- maintain realistic quotas and deadlines
- not value work status as highly as Type A
- appear more organized
- be less driving and more relaxed
- make fewer mistakes
- live longer and have a lower disease record.

Friedman, who studied coronary illness intensively after his own heart attack, suggests that Type A personalities, if they wish to reduce the risk of a coronary, should set

realistic goals, deadlines and quotas, not push themselves and others so hard, learn to use time management
principles, learn what is worth being competitive about
and what isn't, and deal with frustration in a more adult
manner. This would enable them to reduce the amount
of stress which they impose upon themselves.

It would appear that we create our own distress by the
way we perceive things. Yet, despite this, there do exist
certain sources of stress which seem to affect virtually
everybody in a negative way. These will be outlined in
the next chapter.

3 The Sources of Stress

Change

Living has a background, a constant round of daily irritations and rewards, of despairs and of triumphs. However, above this background rise occasional crescendos, identifiable points at which stress reaches such a high level that it demands our attention. There is usually a common element among these apparently diverse crises—change. Whether the change is beneficial or harmful, it poses demands to which our bodies react with the stress response.

It does seem to make a considerable difference whether the crisis is experienced alone or with a large group of people. Often it has been noted that when communities face disasters such as war, physical illness seems largely to disappear, selfishness gives way to altruism, and people tap inner resources of strength far beyond anything they have previously revealed. Conversely, a private crisis may, if the change involved is sufficiently disruptive, cause illness and disease.

Change is seen as the situation most likely to produce anxiety to an individual because it invariably means some disruption of ties or relationships. Even a seemingly insignificant change may re-awaken feelings of helplessness. This is confirmed by the *Life Event Rating Scale* developed by medical researchers Thomas Holmes and Richard Rahe from a study of more than 5,000 patient case histories. These researchers were looking for patterns, for any specific life events, or constellation of life events, which seemed to be related to patient illness. These they found. A number of life change items were found to occur repeatedly, tending to cluster in a brief time period just before the onset of major illnesses. These items, together with a points rating score to indicate the disruptive effect of the change involved, comprise the scale which is given below.

Life Event Rating Scale

Life Event	Score
Death of spouse	100
Divorce	73
Marital separation	65
Prison or mental hospital confinement	63
Death of a close family member	63
Major injury/illness	53
Marriage	50
Being fired	47
Marital reconciliation	45
Retirement	45
Major change in health or behaviour of a family member	44
Pregnancy	40
Sexual difficulties	39
Adding to family (e.g. through birth, adoption, 'oldies' moving in)	39
Major business readjustments	39
Major change in financial state	38
Death of a close friend	36
Changing line of work	36
Major change in number of arguments with spouse	35
Taking on mortgage purchasing home, business etc.	31
Foreclosure on a mortgage or loan	30
Major change in job responsibility	29
Son/daughter leaving home	29

In-law trouble	29
Outstanding personal achievement	28
Wife beginning/ceasing work outside home	26
Beginning/ceasing formal schooling	26
Major change in living conditions	25
Revision of personal habits	24
Troubles with the boss	23
Major change in working hours/conditions	20
Change in residence	20
Changing to a new school	20
Major change in recreation	19
Major change in church activities	19
Major changes in social activities	18
Taking on loan less than $10,000	17
Major change in sleeping habits	16
Major change in number of family get-togethers	15
Major change in eating habits	15
Holidays	13
Christmas	12
Minor violations of law	11

* Based on T. H. Holmes and R. H. Rahe, The Social Re-adjustment Rating Scale, *Journal of Psychosomatic Research*, 11, 1967, pp. 213-18.

Holmes and Rahe claim that if during the course of a year you accumulate a score of more than 300 points, your chance of a serious health problem developing in the next two years is more than 80%. Should your score lie between 150 and 300 points, you have a 50% chance of serious illness in the next two years. The risk drops to 33% for a score of below 150 points.

The Holmes–Rahe scale seems generally applicable regardless of age and race, for it has been tested in many countries with people of different ages to produce similar results. Under all conditions, it is stress derived from the family which provides the highest score events, but it is not always the individual items which cause a person to have a 'danger' score. Because stress is cumulative, the combination of many small items can produce a very high points total.

Holmes argues that the more critical the changes a person experiences, as measured by the Rating Scale, the greater the effort expended in adapting to them. In exerting this effort of adaptation natural resistance to injury and disease is lowered. The longer this struggle to adapt continues, the greater the tendency to withdraw from coping with the environment. The result, if the struggle continues for too long, is apathy or chronic illness. That is why it is so important to try to exert some measure of control over the rate of change you experience.

Jim Graham, recently divorced, could have heeded this advice. He moved from the home in which he had lived for fifteen years, going interstate to a different job and a new house. Reference to the scale indicates that divorce rates 73 points, changing line of work adds 36 points more, and change in residence provides a further 20 points, 129 in all. Other items, such as mortgaging the new home, change in job responsibility, and change in social activities, which all applied in Jim's case, pushed the total higher so he was getting into the danger area. Of course, Holmes' scale is only the expression of a particular theory, and will not be unfailingly right for every person under all circumstances. Still, by embarking on many changes within a short time, Jim is exposing himself to a lot of stress which could, perhaps, be better managed if he spread these over a longer time period.

However, it could be argued that human beings are too complex and different from one another to be measured by a scale as generalized as that of Holmes and Rahe. It is not so much the 'objective' magnitude of a crisis which is important as whether or not the individual concerned actually sees it as a crisis, as something threatening his self-esteem or ability to cope. As we have already seen, it is a person's perception of threat which creates arousal in his or her life. Thus, stress is often a matter of expectation.

Studies of groups such as telephone operators, office secretaries and production line workers indicate that in those who were chronically ill, high stress and repeated crises were related to a life of unfulfilled expectations. These people felt life had treated them badly by somehow preventing them achieving what they were really capable of achieving. Among the other workers who were *not* chronically ill, fulfilled expectations had produced lives in which crises could be handled without too much trauma. Their health, generally, was good. In fact, more than one-third of the healthiest people involved in the studies had endured major changes and deprivations in their lives with no apparent ill-effects.

This basic finding emerges in virtually all research into stress. The variation in reaction to severe stress is very wide, depending to a large extent on the personality of the individual. So Jim Graham, mentioned earlier in this chapter as running up a high score in the Holmes–Rahe Scale, may not necessarily suffer because of it. Jim is flexible in his attachment to other people, groups and goals, and is able to shift readily to other relationships when established ones are disrupted. Thus he will probably handle well the combined changes of his divorce, new job and new home. A less flexible person would probably confirm Holmes' prediction and become seriously ill within the next two years.

It is not only individual personality differences which account for the wide variations in the reaction to severe stress. An understanding of what is happening also plays an important part. Realistic and believable information given before a crisis can lessen shock and adverse after-effects, something well-known to the medical profession. A doctor will often give a patient something to worry about ahead of time so the actual blow, when it comes, will be less upsetting. He sees this as a sort of psychological innoculation designed to build up the patient's resistance. Some evidence suggests that patients prepared for surgery in this way usually adjust better to post-operative stress than ones who worry themselves into a state of high anxiety or expect the operation to be a breeze.

Thus, although the Life Events Rating Scale is valuable in drawing attention to change as the main source of stress in our lives, it does not take account of our own personal capacity for dealing with this stress. Moving from one home to another would, for example, have special difficulties for a family who did not get along well: the blaming, anger and irritation would be extremely arousing. The same move would be far less stressful for a family who got along well, with the individual members supporting and helping each other.

Scales such as that provided by Holmes and Rahe can become self-fulfilling prophecies. That is, we see we have run up several hundred points of change during a year and expect, as a result, to become ill. By thinking in this way, we are likely to make it so. Hypochondriacs do this repeatedly. So do believers in biorhythms.

Recently I conducted a study based on predictions of 'good' and 'bad' days according to the biorhythm charts of my subjects. One group 'knew' when their 'good' and 'bad' days would be, and a comparison of the diaries they kept showed a very close correspondence. On those days predicted as being 'bad' by their biorhythm charts, a lot of unpleasant events happened. Many pleasant things happened on the good days. The second group also kept a diary of what happened to them each day, but they had no knowledge of their supposed 'good' and 'bad' days. Comparison of their diaries and their biorhythm charts showed no relationship at all. It seems we get what we expect.

I am not suggesting you ignore the Holmes–Rahe Scale and its message about the stressful effects of change in your life. Rather, I would advise you to cultivate the art of injecting sufficient variety into your life to provide new experiences, challenge, novelty and stimulus without allowing yourself to be overloaded with an excess of change at any one time.

Jim Graham did permit this overload to take place. Yet, even in his case, perhaps things looked differently to him than to others outside his life situation. Had he remained in his current job, and received there the promotion for which he was due, he would have experienced some role conflict. In most firms, newly promoted people soon notice that old colleagues treat them differently. They are faced with a conflict between keeping old affection and exercising newly bestowed power. This creates considerable stress. Many people in this position attempt to reduce their anxiety by avoiding the use of their power as much as possible and doing everything they can to be liked. Perhaps Jim anticipated this stress-creating problem and negated it by moving to another job. If so, the Life Event Rating Scale would give a misleading reading of his stress level. Invocation of 'the strain of modern living' as a source of arousal can do so too.

The strain of modern living

Obviously, the fast pace and sheer noise of modern life does create stress. So, too, does the loneliness of people who are no longer part of a large family group. Similarly, the rivalry of keeping up with the neighbours is stress-invoking. Yet, 'the increased stress of modern life' is something of a myth, a media creation. Each age provides its own particular sources of arousal and over-arousal. The problem is that we have not yet learned to cope with our particular brand. This, it would seem, is because life has changed more rapidly than have our powers of adaptation. In fact, in many ways, life is less stressful today than it was in the past. It is not just a matter of counting up the number of stresses as if they meant the same thing to everyone. As we have seen, arousal is a personal thing and it depends on how adaptable we are to the particular stresses of modern life.

In shifting from a rural environment to that of the city, we have exchanged ploughs and candlelight for cars, neon signs, television and multi-national corporations. The stresses of the past were primarily harsh, simple and largely predictable, mostly a function of physical threats or deprivations. Our modern stresses are mainly psychological in origin and cumulative in nature, a series of nagging, constant irritations. On a hot summer's day, the refrigerator breaks down. When we go to get our car from the garage, the tyre is flat. Then there are the struggles through crowds, queues at ticket windows, competitions for bus or train seats, interactions with uninterested, faceless bureaucracies, inconveniences of strikes, demonstrations and crime, disturbances of noise, ugliness and crowding. What it all adds up to is a loss of control about which we can do nothing.

Consider a simple little study done in San Francisco a few years ago. Businessmen were asked to wear a pulse counter on their wrists and at set times during the day to note down their pulse rate and what they were doing at the time. These men were battling deadlines, involved in important business deals, arguing with competitors and generally living at a rather frantic pace. Yet the greatest level of arousal they reached, as measured by pulse rate, was when commuting to and from work by car.

Not only executives experience the stress of driving. Signs of moderate to extreme stress are apparent in many drivers. A number of English studies have indicated that in most individuals the average resting heart rate of 70–80 beats a minute rises to a range of 110–115 beats a minute when they drive. The investigators conducting these studies suggest that it is desirable to avoid unnecessary competitive behaviour on the roads, adopting the view that it is better to travel safely than arrive in a rage. So, use of soothing music and cars with automatic transmission are recommended.

Still, individual differences make this advice suitable for some of us and unsuitable for others. I know of several people who find that driving exerts a calming influence, particularly when they can concentrate on actually controlling their vehicle through manual gear changing. This is counter-productive, of course, if they adopt an aggressive 'I must be first' attitude which is reflected in contracted and hunched shoulders, thrust-forward head, tightly clenched teeth, and hands locked on to the steering wheel.

It is not only car travel that is seen as a major source of stress in modern society. Those of us who need to travel frequently by air may suffer also. There are the problems associated with crowding, noise, frustrating delays and, if the journey is a long one, the physical changes associated with the crossing of time zones. Also, should we be away from home for more than a day or two, there is the stress of living out of a suitcase, too little exercise, and possible over-indulgence in eating, drinking and smoking.

The great increase in the speed of transport has placed a strain on our powers of adaptation. It is interesting to note that symptoms produced by 'jet-lag' or 'time-zone fatigue', such as tiredness, insomnia, irritability, digestive disorder, delayed reaction times and impaired judgement, are those usually considered as the early warning signs of stress. These 'jet-lag' symptoms arise not because we are travelling long distances at rapid speeds but because we upset the orderly working of internal clock mechanisms. Humans, like all living organisms, seem to be geared to a 24-hour day, and interruption of our circadian rhythm is disruptive of many of our normal physical patterns. Accordingly, we show evidence of stress.

This is not, however, due entirely to 'jet-lag'. The crowding that is so much a part of modern travel also plays an important role in stress-creation. There is considerable evidence from the animal kingdom that overcrowding causes aggression both within and between species. When these studies are extended to humans, it is possible to observe considerable differences in the behaviour of people who live in towns as compared to the country, and between those who live in large as compared to small cities. In general terms, large city dwellers tend to be more suspicious, hostile, aggressive, time-conscious and destructive. A rather neat little experiment illustrates this destructive aspect.

Two similar cars were abandoned, their bonnets open, in middle class residential areas, one in a large and one in a small American city. In the former, destruction began within five minutes and was complete within eight hours: in the latter, the only event which occurred involved a passer-by lowering the car bonnet to prevent rain wetting the engine.

The effect of overcrowding also reveals itself in the great incidence of illness, both mental and physical, in high-rise flats. An important element here is the isolation felt by people living in such conditions.

Yet real isolation might be something to value. At one time we had only to cope with the problems of our own immediate locality. With the advent of modern lifestyles has come the increased influence of the media. The isolated locality is now the 'global village'—for better or worse. Bad news spreads around the world more quickly than ever. Many people find the constant bombardment of misery—the news of kidnappings and assassinations—highly stressful, wondering why good news is hardly considered news at all.

Many aspects of modern living can produce high levels of stress, though not all people will be similarly affected. This is true, too, of the stress of the workplace.

Work and its stress

In the past, it was relatively easy for a craftsman to derive a sense of satisfaction and personal achievement from his work. This is far less easy for the modern factory or office worker. Even the executive, who is considered by many to do personally fulfilling work, is so far removed from the results of his decisions that he often finds it quite difficult to assess the value of his individual contribution. There is little that is distinctive about his contribution and he knows he could easily be replaced by the firm he serves. Further, human nature being what it is, when he does get feedback from other people, it is likely to be negative, focusing on his mistakes as criticism rather than upon his good decisions as praise.

The result, for many modern workers, is a sense of alienation, of being denied a feeling of satisfaction in the work done. This is a real source of stress, for we all need a sense of status and function, a feeling that what we do matters. As Leo Rosten puts it: 'The purpose of life is not to be happy—but to *matter*, to be productive, to be useful, to have it make some difference that you have lived at all.'

We derive satisfaction from our work if we feel we are doing something that is important in some way. This is particularly so if our efforts are appreciated, for possibly the deepest element in human nature is the craving for appreciation.

Not only must our work seem to serve some useful function, it should also bestow some status upon us. That is why retirement can be a source of great stress. Once a person retires, he loses the status conferred on him through his position in the world of work. His sense of identity gained from this world is gone and he becomes a sort of 'non-person', both in his own eyes and in the eyes of others. This is particularly true of an individual who has spent most of his life in the same organization.

Bill Ross experienced this loss of status on retirement from his job as a boilermaker. He liked his work and took pride in making a good product. Virtually all his working life he had been with the same firm and, upon retirement, found a huge gulf in his life. When asked by others what he did, he could no longer reply, 'I'm a boilermaker.' His reply was really, 'I don't do anything.' Fortunately, Bill realized quickly that it would be personally disastrous for him if his need to belong to something in order to get a sense of purpose and companionship was not met. To keep reasonably busy in a not too demanding way, he engaged in some local voluntary work and attended some adult education evening classes to learn new skills. This activity provided the sense of purpose he had lost through his retirement.

When people invest too much of themselves in their work they become very vulnerable, for if things go wrong in this area they have nothing to fall back on. This is a reason for the stress of the mid-life crisis where an individual realizes he or she has reached a 'ceiling', a position beyond which he or she will probably not advance. This is a choice point: slide into depression because the rest of life looks like being downhill, or look for ways of expanding interests into areas other than work.

Such a broadening of interests might well relieve some of the frustrations of work. Jillian Hadley worked for the Government. A conscientious girl, her attempts to do what she saw as real work, important work, were continually frustrated by the bureaucratic framework within which she had to operate. Obviously, her work was a constant source of stress, for her commonsense practicality was ignored in favour of 'doing it by the book'. Another person, secure within this framework, would experience no such stress.

The work environment furnishes other frustrations also. There is the stress of interruption, when we are trying to concentrate on a particular task. The telephone can be both insistent and intrusive, as can people who drop in to pass the time of day. Pleasant though this can be, it may be very annoying and stress-producing when we are torn between being polite and getting on with the job. This is particularly so when we are attempting to cope with a work overload and the frustration of not being able to do one thing properly because of a multitude of conflicting demands.

This situation may be a function of a lack of clearly defined responsibility. Too many men and women in work of all types are expected to get a job done without being given the power to do it. Anxiety is likely to increase when a person is responsible for the work of others over whom he or she has little control. Responsibility without power of enforcement is a stressful situation, as is role ambiguity. This occurs when people are not sure what they are supposed to do and what is expected of them. Uncertainty breeds anxiety, and it is necessary to provide feedback so people know where they stand, know how well or poorly they are doing a job.

Simply being provided with information about how you are doing can relieve stress. Also, being better informed of what is happening to them may help women cope with their own particular stress situation, one which can seriously affect their work.

Betty Rodgers, normally an efficient secretary, has a 'bad patch' each month during which she makes many mistakes in her work. In addition, she is clumsy around the house, tends to drive her car less carefully than usual, and generally feels headachy and unwell. Betty is suffering from one of the world's most common diseases—pre-menstrual tension. For up to eight days each month, she experiences increased irritability, depression and fatigue. In addition, she feels bloated through fluid retention, and seems to have aches in every joint.

For some time, Betty simply did not realize why she had these 'bad patches', not really being aware they usually occurred a few days before her period, continuing sometimes for a few days afterwards. After reading about pre-menstrual tension and learning that there is increased risk of accidents at this time, Betty took things more easily in the week before her period. When she felt 'off-colour', she attributed it to pre-menstrual tension. Finding a reason for her behaviour helped her immensely. It is a fact of life that when we have found a plausible cause for the things we do, we seem far easier in our minds. We may still behave in the same way, but now we know why, and this seems to relieve us of considerable stress. Knowing why she was irritable and depressed permitted Betty to issue warnings to her family and to her boss to tread warily at certain times. This improved relationships generally.

Actually, as Sartre once commented, 'Hell is other people', so anything that can improve human relationships is worth doing. Probably, more stress is generated through difficulties between people than from any other source. In a marriage, for example, husband and wife have different priorities and often fail to understand each other's problems. To a housewife, her malfunctioning washing machine is just as important as the business deal her husband is bursting to tell her about, yet he is quite unable to see that this could be so. We each tend to become locked up in our own little worlds, impervious to the stresses experienced by our marriage partner. Often this lack of sensitivity results in periods of strained awkwardness relieved by blazing rows to release the tension.

More effort to communicate about situations causing stress can help improve such a relationship, and it is certainly worth doing. Though happily married couples tend to experience less stress-related illness than divorcees, widows and widowers, the same does not hold true for unhappily married couples. It also does not hold true for unhappy work relationships. As Joseph Heller wrote in *Something Happened*:

> In my department, there are six people who are afraid of me, and one small secretary who is afraid of all of us. I have one other person working for me who is not afraid of anyone, not even me, and I would fire him quickly, but I'm afraid of him.

Fear causes stress, according to Heller. Other emotions do, too. Yet, no one really makes us experience our emotions. We do that to ourselves.

Emotional stress

Rarely do we allow ourselves to experience peace of mind, for we are too occupied with immersing ourselves in the five emotions which create stress and tension within us. *Avarice* is one of these, the belief that we need certain things which we probably do not—the 'keeping-up-with-the-times' syndrome—and the feeling that what we depend on will be taken from us. *Ambition* is another. It is fine to set up challenges and want to succeed but it is easy to overdo it, to set unattainable goals and become dissatisfied with ourselves and our activities. A third stress-arousing emotion is *envy*. We irrationally compare what we have achieved with what others have achieved, and use this often invidious comparison as a stick with which to beat ourselves. *Anger* is number four. Ask yourself how often you have allowed others to impose their expectations on you and to control your behaviour—and make you angry as a result. *Pride* is the last of the fatal five emotional underminers of peace of mind. It shows itself in a need to impress both ourselves and others with qualities we really lack. Admitting our human fallibility is much less stressful, yet we find it difficult to do.

With these five emotions operating within us we do not need enemies to create stress for us. We have all the materials ready at hand to do a thorough job on ourselves. Of course we can also add boredom, which is a marvellous way of creating stress. In *A Geography of Consciousness*, William Arkle puts it well when he says:

> We describe things as boring as if it were a quality they possess, like being red or square or shiny. But it is a quality *we* confer on things. And it is because we are only dimly aware of this—of how far we make things boring or fascinating—we waste much of our lives . . . When anticipating some new experience we ask: 'I wonder how interesting it will be?' And if it fails to interest us as much as we expected we become sullen and resentful . . . and because we *automatically* dismiss so much as uninteresting life becomes dull and predictable.

Remember that lack of stimulation can be just as stressful as too much stimulation. If you are low down on the arousal curve through boredom, deliberately 'lift' yourself by pretending things are interesting. As you walk down a familiar street, increase your normal amount of attention, looking at everything as if you were to leave on a long trip and wanted to impress everything on your memory. As you pretend to see things through fresh eyes, your pretence changes into reality and objects and events actually do become more interesting.

Boredom is an aspect of negative thinking, of allowing self-defeating thoughts to control your moods. You feel the way you do now because of the thoughts you have at this moment. Listen to these inner negative thoughts, identify them, see how they are creating stress in your life, and silence them through the techniques outlined in later chapters. You will find many of these negatives present, but perhaps the most damaging as sources of stress can be illustrated by Mary Bowen.

Mary sees everything in black and white. There are no shades of grey, only *all-or-nothing thinking*. During an adult education class, she was criticized once for a poor painting. All her other efforts had been praised. Still, Mary chooses to focus on the one bad performance and regards herself as a failure. She *automatically* discounts positive feedback by simply brushing aside compliments as untrue. By using her *mental filter* she is able to focus exclusively on the negative aspect of the situation and dwell on it to the exclusion of all else.

Because Mary insists on seeing herself as a failure, she *jumps to the conclusion* that everyone else sees her in the same way. She assumes others look down on her because she was criticized for poor work, but she does not check to see how they really do feel. Mary is a 'mind-reader' who 'knows' what other people think. She is a 'clairvoyant' too, looking into the future and seeing only disaster, for she will never, never, never be able to paint well.

Sound familiar? You know people like this? Maybe yourself? Of course—the pattern is very common. Mary is a great *magnifier* of her imperfections and a *minimizer* of her strengths, putting misleading labels on her experiences. She painted one poor picture, so she chose the label of 'I'm a failure'. The label of 'I made a mistake' could fit just as well but she prefers to use ones which are completely negative. In broad terms, what Mary does is to *over-generalize*, to expect continued failure because of one experience.

It is almost as if she fears to think well of herself. As Heller's hero found in *Something's Happening*, fear is a potent source of stress because it relates to a person's self-esteem and the feelings he or she has about being esteemed by others. Most of us are more inhibited and constricted by our own fears and self-doubts than we are by any objective limitations. Often we are afraid to do something because we think we are not good enough or that we cannot really accomplish it when, really, we can do far better than we are doing. I believe we all have tremendous inner resources which remain unused because of the limitations we place on ourselves through our fears and doubts. Vaguely we are aware of this, and the conflict between what we actually do and what we could do if we allowed ourselves is a powerful source of stress.

To a large extent, emotionally induced stress is a matter of control. Tom Perkins, a car salesman, reacts to inner doubts about his own value and worth as a person by making intensive efforts to achieve success. He has become an excellent salesman but he can no longer stop competing now that he has achieved the goal he desired. Tom cannot control his behaviour. He is unable to discriminate between those times when it is appropriate to be competitive, aggressive and pushy, and those times when it is inappropriate. He *has* to compete in virtually every situation in which he finds himself and by so doing places himself under tremendous pressure.

Control is an element in Jillian Rosebery's stress, too. She is constantly clamping a lid on her anger, pretending to herself and to others that it does not really exist. She fears loss of control, being frightened of the terrible things she might do if she expressed her true feelings. It takes a lot of energy to suppress anger and often the results are the stress-induced illnesses of hypertension, headaches and heart trouble.

It is interesting to observe how a group of strangers behave when they meet on a social occasion. For some time they tend to be rather distant and formal, testing each other out. That is, they act as if afraid they might be hurt in some way, yet they know there is little to fear from others socially. Yet, many people feel the need both to defend themselves against others and to control their own feelings in case they hurt or offend someone else.

It is all an illusion. No real threat usually exists. It lies only in the thoughts of the people involved, but these thought processes can trigger anxiety as surely as any physically induced stress. The key to understanding emotional well-being, then, is to realize that just as your body can be mobilized into the stress response by a single thought, so it can be demobilized by another thought.

The common factor in emotionally induced stress is expectation, the belief that something terrible is about to happen. It comes from your imagination. A car accident for example has no reality before it occurs, yet anticipating it, thinking that it could happen, is extremely stressful.

Anticipatory stress, this worry about an impending event, this fear of future catastrophe, seems peculiar to mankind, for animals appear to react instantly to danger when it occurs but to then relax the moment peril is past. Man, on the other hand, is likely to be anxious for weeks before an anticipated crisis arrives and then, instead of relaxing when it is over, continues to relive the event in all its unhappy detail.

When a herd of zebra is chased by a hungry lion, naturally they flee. However, once the lion pulls down one of the weaker members of the herd, the rest of the zebras will contentedly settle down to graze, often within feet of the feeding lion. In a comparable situation, we would spend hours quaking in fear, visualizing the sufferings of our friend, emphathizing with him, and anticipating our own agony should we be the next to be attacked.

It is our imagination which causes us such stress, stress which is really quite unnecessary in that it does not help us cope any better with the situations confronting us. While waiting to take a driving test, for instance, nervousness may cause our hands to shake, our breathing to speed up, and our muscles to become so tense we perform far below our capacity.

We can of course induce stress in ourselves in ways

other than that of anticipating the worst. *Time stress*, the feeling that something must be done before a deadline, that time is running out, is very common. So too, is *situational stress*, in which we may be faced with a situation that is threatening and, partially, at least, beyond our control, and *encounter stress* in which our anxieties about dealing with other people are paramount. Often we can experience a sense of overload in being around other people, even when they are quite friendly, and, as a marvellous antidote to stress, it is delightful to retire into privacy and isolation when the need is there.

It is amazing how often, though, we do not permit ourselves this time to be alone with ourselves. Perhaps this may be due to self-imposed obligations. We undertake crash projects, accept deadlines, agree to do challenging tasks—and then become our own slave drivers, urging ourselves on and becoming anxious at the thought of not performing as well as we think we should. We make our deadlines sacred, something to be achieved at all costs. Although we normally associate such behaviour with business, it is quite common in other areas too. I'm sure you can think of many housewives, for example, who martyr themselves on the altar of household chores which 'must' be done.

A way out is to revise our view of what constitutes an obligation, keeping those we can reasonably keep, negotiating those which are no longer feasible, and declining to make those that seem unreasonable. It is often useful, too, when we are busy telling ourselves what we 'must' do, to ask: 'What would happen if I didn't do this?' Usually the answer is 'Nothing.' Such an answer serves to confirm that we are creating our own stress, and by so doing, exposing ourselves to illnesses we need not have.

4 The Stress–Illness Link

A model of stress

Much of the material so far presented may be summarized in the form of the following diagrammatic model.

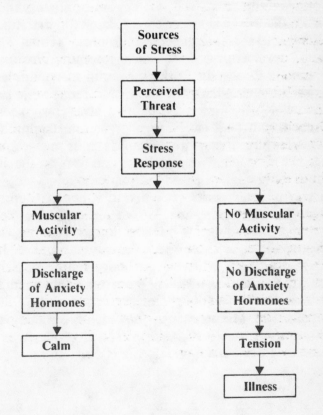

As we have seen, the stress response readies the body for fight or flight. This muscular activity dissipates the chemicals poured into the bloodstream and permits the body to return to a state of relative calm. However, should muscular activity be impossible, these chemicals accumulate and during a long period of stress a state of chronic tension ensues. It is this constant tension which has been linked to the development of a number of diseases.

If blood pressure, for example, remains high and blood vessels are constricted, cardiovascular disease in the form of heart attacks or strokes may result. Should the stomach remain with the reduced blood supply which is part of the body's response to stress, and the mucous membrane of the gut engorges, there will be digestive disorders such as constipation or diarrhoea, duodenal and stomach ulcers, and colitis. If the lungs continue, over a period, to strive for more air, over-breathing will occur, bringing with it giddiness, faintness, and problems for asthma sufferers. The skin changes which are associated with the stress response, if prolonged, can lead easily to allergies and rashes for people who have a constitutional weakness in this area. Similarly headaches, backaches, and muscle pain are likely to result if the body is maintained in a state of tension for long periods. When the body reacts to environmental demands, the antiinflammatory mechanism is subdued. If this reaction is present for an extended period, a person becomes more susceptible to infection.

Note that it is when the body is kept in a state of readiness for action over long periods that illness becomes likely. Momentary crises which are coped with quickly provide no such problem, for the body returns to a state of calm quite rapidly. It is also important to realize that stress is not the only factor involved in the various disorders mentioned above. Nor may it necessarily be the main one. However, there exists considerable evidence to suggest that it does play a significant part in triggering off many illnesses.

Stress-related illness

Stephanie Marlowe suffers from chronic anxiety about herself, her life and her surroundings. She sees danger everywhere. Yet she is unaware of her stress—she has lived with it for so long, it is simply part of her life. If she is to manage it more effectively, she needs to become more aware of her state, realizing that her inability to relax, impatience, irritability, digestive problems, rapid-fire speech and lack of a sense of humour are all indicators of the stressful life she is leading.

Stephanie unconsciously attempts to manage her stress by becoming ill. Her sickness removes her from a situation she cannot handle, while at the same time it allows her to think of herself as a sick person rather than as one who cannot solve her problems. By acting in this way, Stephanie transforms an unacceptable mental state into a socially acceptable illness. Because she has used this form of stress management for many years, Stephanie is a chronic hypochondriac.

Other people may not always become sick when under pressure but it does appear that stress is clearly a cause, if not *the* cause, of headaches, backaches, ulcers and high blood pressure. Some specialists have estimated that up to 90% of headaches arise from contraction of the neck and head muscles. This tension derives from a readiness to spring into some form of physical action which never takes place. In some circumstances, such as driving in heavy traffic or studying for an examination, we seem to brace ourselves as if we are carrying a heavy load, tightening the shoulder muscles as well as those of the neck and face. Back pain is usually the result.

A rise in blood pressure is one of the normal, inevitable reactions to stress. When the threat causing the stress response passes, the blood pressure usually drops. However, if the state of alarm continues in the form of conscious or unconscious fear, hostility, anxiety or frustration, this does not happen and the blood pressure remains at the higher level.

Cholesterol level, too, can rise as a physical reaction to stress, especially where some form of emotional conflict or frustration is involved. In fact, it is possible to create such a rise by simply talking about subjects which a person perceives as stressful.

The relationship between stress and disease is an interactional one. Every disease causes a certain amount of stress because it imposes upon the body demands for adaptation. Conversely, stress plays some part in the development of every disease, its effects being added to the specific changes characteristic of the particular disease. That is why it is very important to identify the causes of our tension and anxiety, whether it be a family member, our boss, our overemphasis on always being right, or our acceptance of too many new responsibilities. We can then work to reduce their effect upon us. This approach, in the long term, is likely to be more fruitful than using drugs to mask the symptoms of our stress, for ill-health is largely a failure of adaptation, of not modifying our way of life to better cope with the demands of our environment.

The importance of stress as a contributory factor in illness is emphasized by the oft-repeated estimate that probably three-quarters of all complaints treated in general medical practice are stress-related. That is, those symptoms which cause people to visit their doctor might not have occurred at all, or would have been less severe, had the stress not been present. Unfortunately, it is easy to accept the idea that illness-creating stress is an unavoidable consequence of the pace and complexity of western life, and that there is not much point in trying to overcome the problem.

If we believe that much illness is created by stress, and that the response to environmental demands depends upon the perception of each individual, upon the way he or she sees the world, then sickness begins in the mind. Therefore, it is the mind that needs to be healed. Stephanie, the hypochrondriac mentioned earlier in this chapter, will continue to be constantly ill until she is able to abandon her deluded ideas that the world of distress she experiences is real rather than a product of her own beliefs about herself and the 'threats' of her surroundings. Until she seriously questions her belief system and the way she is choosing to think, Stephanie will make very little progress towards reducing the stress in her life.

Many health experts believe that the ability to handle stress is the single most important asset a person can have in combating illness, for it is becoming increasingly clear that fear, anxiety, confusion, frustration and insecurity are emerging as the causes of more disease than bacteria and viruses. Major infectious diseases have been controlled by antibiotics, vaccines and public health measures, but the medical profession has not been as successful in the prevention of stress-related illness. Modern doctors usually treat stress by suggesting the distressed patient talks to someone about his or her problem, takes drugs, or has an operation.

About one-fifth of all prescriptions given to patients in America, the United Kingdom and most other Western countries are for sleeping pills, tranquillizers or anti-depressants. It seems our greatest international drug addiction problem is not one of teenagers taking marijuana or heroin, but middle-agers taking tranquillizers. The comment has been made, with considerable justification, that if all the people on tranquillizers were banned from driving or operating machinery, the world's economy would collapse overnight. Often, unfortunately, patients begin their addiction to prescribed drugs in hospitals.

Apart from prescribed drugs, alcohol and tobacco are commonly seen as the means whereby people under pressure can gain relief. Unfortunately, many patients who develop cancer of the lungs or cirrhosis of the liver have become victims of their own solutions. It is true that about half of all illness has a direct psychological basis. It is equally true to say that about half of the remainder is caused by remedies, such as smoking, drinking alcohol and using over-the-counter drugs which have been prescribed by the sufferers themselves.

These remedies can help, at least in the short term. Many smokers, for instance, claim tobacco helps them cope with difficult situations, manage their relationships with other people better, and control bad temper more effectively. The problem is, though, that smoking seems to be a form of slow-motion suicide, for approximately 40% of smokers can be expected to die through lung cancer, chest infection and heart disease as a result of their addiction.

It is interesting to note that United States Navy pilots and navigators taken prisoner by the North Vietnamese during the Vietnam war were healthier when examined after their release than a similar group of non-captured fliers. Doctors felt this was due to the prisoners having been kept physically fit through exercise, and having been deprived of alcohol, excessive fats, tobacco and stress-producing paperwork.

Our indulgence in drugs designed to relieve our stress indicates how common the feelings of anxiety, tension and pressure are. As previously described, anxiety mobilizes our glands, muscles and mechanisms of defense for action. Often, when caught in conflict, we end up doing nothing, permitting the energy mobilized in our bodies to turn against us in destructive ways. Sugerman and Freeman, in *The Search for Serenity*, put it beautifully when they say: 'We simmer in the broth of all the exotic hormones and chemicals which have been produced as an end to action.'

It is this stewing in our own juices which generates all manner of physical reactions. In fact, once we can express our underlying feelings, perhaps through weeping or an explosion of anger, symptoms such as skin rashes or gastrointestinal problems may simply disappear. The habit of doing nothing when under stress can be very destructive. We are better off doing *something*, which is the reason I suggest exercise as a valuable antidote to stress (see chapter 6).

Diagrammatically, Melhuish expresses the relationship between stress and illness in this way.

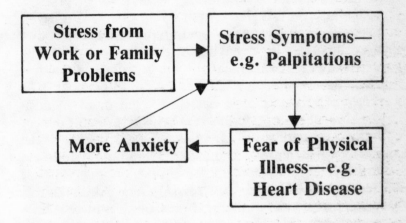

It's a vicious circle, one which an acquaintance of mine, Alec Blair, experienced in classic form. He and his wife, Lynn, were not getting along well, talking about a possible separation. In addition, Alec had been given increased work responsibilities which were worrying him a lot. One night he woke from a deep sleep, sweating and frightened. He realized his heart was beating quite irregularly, sometimes racing, at other times slowing down. Immediately his fears of a heart attack surfaced, yet there was no pain involved at all. Just as suddenly as the symptom had appeared, it vanished. Alec's heart beat returned to normal and he felt quite comfortable.

The next day he had a medical check-up. Apparently

his heart was quite healthy. However, the seed of doubt had been planted. Also, Alec remembered the stories of patients going to their doctors, being assured their hearts were sound, and then suffering a heart attack on the way home. Through his fear, Alec increased his anxiety. Because he was feeling fearful and anxious, his stress symptoms became more pronounced—more irregular heartbeats, more palpitations. Accordingly, his tension further increased.

Fay Hammond is another person locked into the same vicious circle. Every symptom she observes in herself is a sign of cancer. Her fear increases her stress level, generates further physical symptoms, and she becomes more anxious. By behaving in this way, Fay may be increasing the chances that she will get cancer. Chemical pathologist, Malcolm Carruthers, in his book, *The Western Way of Death*, has stated that many medical experts suspect long-term stress helps to promote cancer in that its depressive effect is believed to affect the body's self-defense mechanism, the immune system. He feels evidence exists indicating that, in many cases, cancer occurs following a stressful event. Although this cancer-stress link is still largely speculative, there is little doubt of the link between stress and heart attacks.

Heart attacks and the Type A individual

According to Carruthers, the main cause of the heart disease plague affecting civilized man is the imbalance between his mental and physical activity. This results in an inappropriate chemical response to the sedentary stresses of modern life. Over a period of years, the consequent unnecessary mobilization of sugar and fats leads to a narrowing of the arteries supplying blood to the heart and to promoting the formation of blood clots. Finally, a heart attack occurs.

Heart attacks, too, are a likely response to excessive competitive drive and the meeting of deadlines. In creating the clock we may well have created an instrument for our own destruction, for it becomes easy to see time as the enemy against whom we are doomed to fight throughout our lives. Yet, many people turn time into a challenge, creating eustress by regarding it as a spur enabling them to achieve their best work under deadline pressure.

The clearest link between heart attacks and stress lies in the research done on the Type A, hard-driving personality who is particularly prone to this illness and to whom incessant stress may well be the mainstay of his or her character, Rob Cole, General Manager of an insurance company, is the embodiment of the Type A individual. A volcanic struggler, he bustles—his aggression seething just below the surface. His table-pounding and nervous facial tic indicate this inner turmoil. With an habitual sense of time urgency, he is a chronic hurrier, constantly trying to accomplish too much in the time he allows himself. In sport, discussion and card games, he is an aggressively combative challenger. Naturally, when forced to wait in a queue, he is in anguish. He loathes long books, repetitious jobs and situations which result in inefficiency. Rob is a real one-man band, often striving to do a number of different things at once.

This Type A pattern is often thought of as being the province of the middle-class executive alone, but it is quite common among city dwellers of virtually every occupation and class. Rob, being an A type, tends to abuse his body, taking little exercise, eating rich foods, and drinking and smoking heavily. Friedman and Rosenman, who developed the concept of the Type A personality, suggest that such people are, on average, almost three times more likely to suffer coronary disease than the more relaxed Type Bs. It seems striving is the essence of their lives and they would sooner die than fail.

Type A people often fail to realize that the pressures

they feel come from within themselves rather than from external situations. As long as they believe that stress is something 'out there', rather than something they do to themselves, they will continue to kill themselves with heart attacks far more frequently than would be the case if they learned to moderate their lifestyle somewhat. For it is possible to manage stress, or more correctly, distress. We can see this by referring again to the stress model and making certain additions.

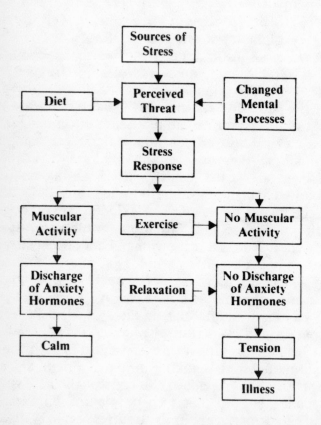

Changing the way we choose to think about events in the environment can reduce the amount of threat we see. So, too, can certain dietary measures. By reducing our perception of threat, we activate our stress response less frequently and remain calm for longer periods. When the stress response is present we can exercise to provide the muscular activity necessary for the body to release the energy it has mobilized. Alternatively, we can relax in order to promote the dissipation of the chemicals released in the body through our reaction to environmental demands. These approaches to stress management all work. Let us now consider how they produce their beneficial results.

5 Managing Stress

A general approach to handling stress

In earlier chapters I have attempted to emphasize that the perception of stress is very much an individual matter. Therefore, the first step in coping more effectively is to identify the sorts of stress which affect you in negative ways. Are the goals you set for yourself and your family too difficult to achieve? Is your work monotonous, or do you suffer from constant deadlines? Does the clock control your life so that being busy is more important than being happy? Becoming aware of what you see as stress and how you react to it will help you decide how best to handle the problem.

Perhaps you will decide to reduce the family stress level by bringing difficulties out in the open and talking about them, by setting priorities on how money is to be spent, and by organizing a fair distribution of tasks between family members. Maybe you'll stop trying to do more than one thing at a time, change the way you think about the clock and find more opportunities to do things you enjoy doing. It is possible you will choose to slow down a little, talking more quietly, listening more attentively to others, and adopting a pace suitable to the sort of person you are. You may even wish to get up half an hour earlier so you can begin the day in a more leisurely fashion, perhaps even taking a walk before or after breakfast, and generally avoiding the rush to get off to work.

It is necessary to examine your own situation and

come up with your own solutions, hopefully assisted by the ideas in this and later chapters. Such help should prove valuable, for, as we have seen, the forms of escape from stress chosen by most people often generate undesirable side effects. These include frequent eating, especially of sweet foods, drinking alcohol, smoking, drinking coffee, colas or other high caffeine drinks, using marijuana or other mind-altering drugs, using prescription drugs as tranquillizers or pain killers, using sleeping pills, withdrawing psychologically, behaving like a robot, self-destructive behaviour, and lashing out at others, displacing anxiety and anger upon them.

Very few consciously selected forms of stress avoidance have the potential to constructively reduce arousal. Those which can achieve this end include learning to relax the body physically; exercise; re-engineering pressure situations, either through getting out of the situation completely, departing for long enough to unwind physically and mentally, or changing your attitude so it appears less threatening, and teaching yourself to react less intensely to the requirements of your environment.

There is no need to seek ways of escaping from stress altogether. Rather, it is a matter of *developing a range of coping techniques* which can be used as the occasion demands, of finding out how to balance the episodic stress we experience with substantial periods of recuperation and repair. Balance is a key principle of low-stress life patterns. It involves a proper proportion of work and play, challenge and ease, stress and relaxation, striving and taking it easy, companionship and solitude, exercise and rest, discipline and self-indulgence. Training yourself for change is also involved so that you occasionally vary your routines, perhaps reading a different newspaper, taking a different route to work, trying a new hobby, or getting up at a different time. Such deliberate variation of life can provide an immediate tonic and act as an 'insulation', protecting you to some extent against the time when change is thrust on you.

Another key principle of a low-stress life is adaptation. This is a matter of taking things in your stride, of observing what is happening and choosing to react in non-stressful ways, of allowing provocations and annoyances to disappear once they are over. It includes the ability to relax and unwind, to reduce your level of internal arousal when you want to. Actually, the best way of avoiding harmful stress is to select an environment, including spouse, boss, and friends, which is in line with your inner preferences and to find an activity which you enjoy. Not easy to achieve, of course, but only thus can you eliminate the need for the frustrating constant readaptation which is the major cause of distress.

Less idealistically, avoidance of distress can often be achieved through diversion from one activity to another. This is more relaxing than complete rest. Actually, few things are as frustrating as complete inactivity, the lack of any stimulus or challenge to which you can react. It is interesting to note that among patients with an incapacitating incurable disease, those who seek relief through complete rest seem to suffer most. This would appear to be because they are unable to avoid constantly thinking about their hopeless future. On the other hand, those patients who manage to go on being active for as long as possible appear to gain strength through coping with the many little tasks of daily life, their minds being diverted from more miserable considerations.

Change is possible. Some of the patients mentioned above are able to become more active, once they realize that their complete rest solution is not providing the results they want. Friedman, co-author of *Type A Behaviour and Your Heart*, is a specific example of a person who set out to change quite deliberately. After a heart attack, he decided to change from being a Type A personality to becoming a Type B personality. To this end he took to wearing tweedy old sports jackets, moved from the city to a placid suburb, gave up cocktail parties, his pipe and membership of committees, read books he could not possibly rush through, and purposely allotted more time to various activities than they might appear to require. Friedman commenced getting up 15-20 minutes earlier in the mornings, took breaks for day-dreaming while at work, looked out the window at the view, missed heavy meals and used the time for walking or browsing instead. That is, he slowed down his pace and re-ordered his priorities, believing that he could best avoid heart attacks by losing excess weight, stopping smoking, taking regular exercise and learning how to relax.

Friedman was, in fact, making more use of the three mutually supporting factors of relaxation, diet and exercise, the wellness triad as they have been called. He realized that he could, for example, overcome the excessive eating that often results from tension and strain by either taking some exercise before meals or, should that be impossible, relaxing for a few minutes before eating.

Type B personalities tend to relieve pressure by breaking the work routine, pursuing outside interests and providing for rest and relaxation during the day. Friedman's behaviour was moving him in this direction away from his previous Type A pattern of trying to overcome stress by working harder. However, the changes he made could not have taken place if he had been unaware of his own behaviour. As most stress is self-induced, we can develop lower levels of arousal through being alert for situations likely to create distress and by choosing how we can respond to those situations in non-stressful ways.

Self-awareness

The cornerstone on which to construct a strategy of

coping is to accept human conflict and tension as an inevitable aspect of existence. The key to choosing the most effective ways of dealing with such stress is self-awareness. Be aware of your physical and emotional reactions by recognizing the signs of stress such as sweating palms, racing heart and churning stomach. Determine whether yours is a Type A lifestyle marked by constant hurry, attempts to achieve more and more in less and less time, and uneasiness when you are sitting doing nothing.

Self-awareness also includes identifying the circumstances producing stress, such as work overload, being stuck in a traffic jam, or an over-spending spouse, and then deciding on your most appropriate response. It is this pause for reflection before acting which can be so valuable, yet often we react instantly, more like machines than human beings. We can decide to 'fight', perhaps by shouting at our spouse or a subordinate who errs, to 'take flight', by leaving the room for a while, or to adapt and accept the situation.

Successful management of stress is all about choices. Stress can be greatly magnified if we lack insight into our own behaviour, not recognizing the origins of the problem within ourselves and blaming external situations and other people. For years, Ken Moore suffered from 'nervous stomach' and severe headaches. These he regarded as normal health problems. However, after reading an earlier book of mine, *The Healing Factor: A Guide to Positive Health*, he began, consciously, to 'listen' to his own body, to become aware of the messages it was attempting to communicate.

Ken realized that the knotted sensation in his abdomen, the irregular bowel movements and the bloated feelings usually preceeded occasions on which he would be 'on trial' in one way or another. He felt this way before a golf match, as he did before visiting a client to whom he wanted to sell insurance. Once Ken realized the existence of this long-standing pattern, he found his attacks of 'nervous stomach' became less frequent. So, too, did headaches, which were closely related to his worrying about deadlines he had to meet.

Simply identifying these patterns helped Ken. He got to know his normal reactions to stress and accepted them as part of himself, becoming familiar with his physical sensations, his emotional responses, and his escape behaviour such as smoking and drinking increased amounts of alcohol. Taking this concept a little further, Ken deliberately listed his strengths and weaknesses, clarifying the important goals in his life so that the gap between the person he was and the person he would like to be was not too great. Often the goals we set ourselves are unrealistic, but we are simply not aware of this. We create such a large gap between our actual and desired selves that we place ourselves under constant pressure to achieve the unachievable. Once this is realized, as in Ken's case, it is possible to modify goals in order to reduce this pressure.

Ken's wife, Lorraine, saw the change in her husband as a result of his increased self-awareness. She, too, became increasingly conscious of her own responses. Her main indicator of stress was fatigue: 'I'm so tired all the time', a case of too much energy out and too little energy in. 'What am I doing,' she asked herself, 'to cause this sapping of my energy?' 'Nothing' was the answer. Lorraine was bored. Once she had done her basic chores around the house, she found it difficult to fill in time. She was under-aroused, under-stimulated—a condition revealing itself, in her case, as constant tiredness.

To build up her personal energy resources, Lorraine experimented with three different methods. One was exercise, seen often as the perfect outlet for the accumulated frustrations, anxieties and tensions of everyday living. In particular, she took up badminton, an activity that made her perspire and her heart and breathing rate increase considerably. Such vigorous exercise often provides an excellent antidote to the stress of under-stimulation.

Lorraine also tried 'time-out activities' such as meditation, short naps and yoga exercises. These, she felt, would provide something different from her normal activities. However, they were not different enough and she found they did little to relieve her fatigue.

Her third method of getting away from the home environment for breaks, even if quite short in duration, did help a lot. She and Ken began going away for weekends together and this seemed to provide an escape valve for both of them.

Like Lorraine, you will find there is a preferred way for you to cope with stress once you become aware that you are showing the signs of tension and strain. This might be physical, such as jogging or gardening; emotional, such as hugging your children, laughing or crying; social, such as telephoning a friend or going out for lunch; intellectual, such as reading or listening to music; or spiritual, such as meditating or admiring the beauty of the world around you. The key to choosing an *effective energizer* is that it must assist you to develop a different perspective on your life. If you usually turn to physical exercise when stressed, try doing a cross-word puzzle instead. Should watching television be your preferred anti-tension behaviour, try running around the block. There is no one right way. Experiment to find what you can do to help yourself attain that optimum level of arousal where you feel good, free of the physical and mental signs of stress.

Seek your own stress level, decide if you are a Type A racehorse or a Type B turtle and live accordingly. Choose your own goals, making sure they are really yours and not those imposed on you by others who feel they know what is best for you. Look after yourself by being necessary to others, for this gives a sense of purpose or importance to your existence—and do find out more about your own needs. Considering the following may help you do so:

1 Perhaps I no longer need to . . .
2 Maybe I need to . . . some more.
3 Possibly, sometime soon, I need to . . .
4 Perhaps, once again, I need to . . .
5 Maybe, sometimes, I need to . . .

The first of these clarifies what you would like to change: 'perhaps I no longer need to keep the house always spotlessly clean.' The second clarifies what you would like to keep: 'Maybe I need to develop more interests outside of my work.' Clarification of future goals comes from the third: 'Possibly, sometime soon, I need to learn to meditate.' A resource from the past comes from the fourth: 'Perhaps, once again, I need to go on vacation with my family.' An area where more flexibility is needed reveals itself in the final question: 'Maybe, sometimes, I need to praise my workmates, subordinates and family.'

Once you become aware of your own stress response and what you are doing to impose pressure upon yourself, you are in a position to modify your mental attitude and, by so doing, reduce the threat you perceive in your environment.

The modification of your mental attitude

As we have seen, our attitude determines whether we perceive any experience as pleasant or unpleasant. Adoption of the former can convert a negative stress into Selye's eustress. As the Austrian-Hungarian folk proverb has it, 'Imitate the sundial's ways, count only the pleasant days.' This is done by exercising control over our imagination and thoughts, for this means control over our actions.

Mary Temple is a chronic worrier. She has become this way through practice. When whatever she is worrying about is resolved, without a pause she immerses herself in her next worry. Naturally, she casts an aura of stressful gloom over all unfortunate enough to be in contact with her. On any day, Mary could choose to dwell on pleasant aspects of her life, for she has these in abundance—a pleasant husband, intelligent children, comfortable home, no money worries—but she does not do so. Rather, she broods on the sad aspects, the things that are wrong. Most of these are quite trivial—an ache here and there, a dented car, disrespect shown by a neighbour, hot weather—but Mary chooses to fill her thoughts with these, worrying and fretting. She is like the first of Frederick Langbridge's men in his oft-quoted couplet:

Two men look out through the same bars:
One sees the mud, and one the stars.

Mary has acquired her particular emotional set through habit. Through constant practice she has become tense, miserable and depressed. However, she could also, if she wished, practise being optimistic, relaxed and confident. She has elected to fill her mind with negative emotions such as grief, remorse, anger, resentment and fear rather than the positive ones of hope, joy and cheerfulness.

This is a choice we all have. True, even with the most optimistic, positive attitude in the world we will have to endure occasional disappointments, failures and setbacks, but there is no need for us to make such visitors into permanent house guests. As the Chinese proverb has it, 'You cannot prevent the birds of sorrow from flying over your head, but you can prevent them from building nests in your hair.' Unpleasant stress-creating memories gradually fade away provided they are not constantly recalled to mind. As long as we deliberately halt the process of constant recollection, time alone wipes clean the slate. Much stress could be avoided in this way, by allowing the past to bury its mistakes. So many real and imaginary problems would simply disappear if we did not keep refabricating them in our minds, yet it would be difficult to convince someone like Mary that this could be so.

She would find it somewhat peculiar if she was told that many of the things she worried about could be relabelled, that she could choose to see a promise in every problem. Robert Harrison, an executive who participated in one of my workshops, was a person who consistently operated in this way. Quite early in his career, he was placed in a situation which he lacked the experience to handle. Yet there was no one in the organization to whom he could turn for help. Although Robert found this a very stressful situation, he learned a great deal from it and still looks upon it as one of the most valuable experiences of his life because he treated it as a challenge, and found that distress became eustress.

Deadlines are often stressful, yet Robert and others like him use them, not only to get a job done on time but to actually provoke a better thinking process, for the added pressure seems to put many people in top gear. They rise to the challenge. Sometimes, too, in his executive capacity, Robert uses stress deliberately in order to force a person to perform beyond his expectations. His experience has been that once this enhanced performance had been accomplished, the person was then able to repeat it with increased confidence in himself. Some would find such treatment a source of distress; many others find it pushes them beyond the limitations they have imposed on themselves into a feeling of eustress.

It is very much a matter of the messages we give ourselves whether we experience distress or eustress. Are we able to give ourselves positive messages when things are going wrong or do we catastrophize and worry? Do we want to lift ourselves up or put ourselves down? If we want to help ourselves, instead of being our own worst enemies, we can choose to tell ourselves the things that make us feel good rather than the things that make us feel bad. Why should we inflict pain on ourselves when it is just as easy to give ourselves joy?

Mary, the expert worrier referred to earlier, uses a form of negative self-hypnosis to convince herself that she is a terrible person who does awful things. Because she believes she cannot be any different, all sorts of things are impossible for her. If she does something well, she rarely dwells on it, praising and encouraging herself. Rather, she either ignores it or finds some way of belittling what she has done.

In *This Will Drive You Sane*, Bill Little describes people like Mary, commenting that 'with effort, problems can be created, guilt induced, neuroses nurtured'. He goes on to outline eight principles of problem production through which out-of-step people, that is, those who are happy and well-adjusted, can become as miserable as everyone else. They are worth looking at, these *eight principles*, because people who practise them create great distress for themselves.

Firstly, become a snowballer. Realize that if you face problems when they first appear they are likely to vanish. Therefore, always allow problems to become firmly established by letting them snowball. That is, when it is past time to do something about a problem, wait a little longer.

The second principle suggests that you learn to say, 'This is my problem', blaming yourself for virtually everything that happens to you. For example, someone does not like you. Assume the fault is entirely yours, refusing to even contemplate the idea that the problem may lie partly or wholly with the other person.

This is an adjunct of principle number three which advises you to take a negative focus, telling yourself that you are *always* mistreated and misunderstood by *everyone*. Be aware of the intrusion of happy thoughts. Should you think of anything good about yourself, quickly focus on a related weakness.

Expecting bad things is the fourth principle, because your very expectation influences your behaviour to create the negative situation. You go to a party expecting to have a bad time. You stand alone, keeping well away from the action, and later bemoan the fact that no one would have anything to do with you.

Principle number five is never giving a damn about others and disliking yourself as heartily as possible. You can then tell yourself, 'I'm no good, therefore nobody else is any good either.'

Another good distress maker is always to set your goals out of reach. That is the sixth principle. Little quotes the example of a woman taking two university subjects, learning to play the piano, caring for two children and two sick relatives, and working at a regular job. She insisted she would not be satisfied with anything less than distinctions in her two university subjects. She is obviously a real expert at the distress game.

So, too, are people who create barriers to understanding. They never compliment anyone, avoid any semblance of an encouraging remark, and continually nag, complain and fuss. Such people are practising principle number seven. While doing so they may also embrace the eighth principle by becoming martyrs, issuing statements such as 'I work my fingers to the bone and no one cares.'

Little is poking fun at the sort of people who do the things described in his eight principles, but he is right. People do behave in these ways, creating a lot of distress for themselves which need never have existed. Actually, one very popular way of doing this, which he fails to mention, is the constant repetition of our troubles. For years, psychologists, psychiatrists and the media, particularly in the form of women's magazines, have urged us to talk our problems out. This is all right up to a point but the constant repetition of problems to virtually everyone we meet not only bores our listeners but also creates mental images which create tension.

A more positive attitude is likely to reduce tension. When you assess something or somebody, look for the good points. In particular, accept people as they are with all their shortcomings instead of finding fault—critics tend to be more tense and nervous than other more tolerant beings. Also, it is not a bad idea to keep clear of critics, preferring to mix with more positive people rather than those who create a stressful atmosphere around themselves.

Positive people tend to laugh a lot, being able to accept and appreciate the incongruities of life. Usually, much of their laughter is directed at themselves, a personality characteristic which enables them to tackle problems from new perspectives. Laughter, once described as the sunshine of the soul, is one of the best ways of dispelling tension. The short, explosive exhalations alter the breathing pattern as the facial muscles contract, puffing away the tension. As a psychiatrist once commented, 'I've seldom been called upon to help a person who had a sense of the ridiculous, and I've never had to treat anyone who could really laugh at himself.'

Rarely, also, do psychiatrists have to treat people who adopt a positive attitude to worrying. The old slave lady in *Gone with the Wind* expressed such an approach when she said, 'Thursday's muh worryin' day. Ever' Thursday, ah sets down fo' a little while, and ah worries about things. Then I don't have to worry no mo' for the rest of da week.' Very sensible. So, too, is the idea of making two lists, one of those things which normally worry you but about which you can do nothing, and the other of the worries that you can do something about. Whenever you think of something on the first list, imagine a bright, red flashing light in your mind saying STOP, and divert your thoughts towards constructive thinking about something on the second list.

This is a matter of recognizing unhelpful dead-end thoughts and substituting more constructive ones. The thought-stopping process mentioned above is one way of accomplishing this. Because the word STOP has powerful connotations, 'seeing' it in the mind as an image, or 'hearing' it shouted to yourself when you are thinking in self-destructive ways creates a pause which may be used for the substitution of a self-enhancing thought. It is helpful to have a store of positive topics and images available to replace the thoughts that bother you.

This thought-switching translates easily into action. Imagine you arrive late at the airport having been delayed by heavy traffic. You miss your plane. Instead of agonizing over what has happened, switch off these unhelpful thoughts. Accept the reality of the situation, that you have no means of changing what has happened, and concentrate on what to do next. For example, you could present your problem to the reservations clerk and ask him for suggestions. What you need to do is let go the stress-provoking worrying over something you cannot alter, face the facts, and ask yourself what choices you have.

Taking purposeful action is one way of banishing fears, doubts and crippling indecision. So often it is non-specific worries that create stress, the free-floating anxiety which may be quite unrelated to any outside event but which causes a person to peer at the world through a miasma of gloom. Living in the present, becoming absorbed in whatever you are doing, can divert your mind from this anxiety. Building up a treasure house of restful thoughts in your mind can accomplish the same result, as can deliberately attempting to find, say, four good things in every adverse event you face.

These 'techniques' for the better handling of worry are all aspects of a positive attitude of mind, as is the concept of learning to live with little. The more we have, the more anxious we are at the realization that, at any time, we might lose our props. Something might happen to remove the comfortable home, the car and the nice clothes. Further, we may not even enjoy what we do have, because we are constantly yearning for something else.

Practising the art of acceptance can help overcome the distress created in this way. Savouring what we have is important. Logan Pearsall Smith puts it like this: 'There are two things to aim at in life; first to get what you want; and, after that, to enjoy it. Only the wisest of mankind achieves the second.'

Discontent seems so much part of us, fanned by an advertising industry which is aimed at making us dissatisfied with whatever we have. Nagging discontent is an ever-present source of stress, so learning to live with what we have, and enjoying it, can be very helpful in reducing the pressure on us. Acting in this way can make a positive contribution to our health. Migraine sufferers, for example, are often so preoccupied with their struggle to attain higher goals that they rarely provide themselves with 'resting points of contentment' to enjoy what they have achieved.

Positive thinkers are kind to themselves; negative thinkers are hard on themselves. The irrationality of the self-destructive approach is revealed by David Burns in this quotation from *Feeling Good: The New Mood Therapy*. 'If a famous visitor came to stay with you, would you insult him? Would you peck away at his weaknesses and imperfections. Of course not. You would do everything you could to make your guest feel comfortable. Now—why not treat yourself like that? Do it all the time!'

Be kind to your family, too. Much of our stress stems from family problems, so handling these more positively is likely to help you live more peacefully. Limit arguments to current events instead of raking up old scores. They are part of the past and bringing them into the present creates unhelpful tension. Refuse to use absolute terms such as 'You *always* . . .', 'You *never* . . .'. During an argument it is useful to stop and ask yourself, 'What am I trying to achieve?' If the answer is to inflict pain or to impose punishment you might choose to stop the row. You can't? No, it is not easy—but this ability to pause for self-observation is vital if you are to manage stress more successfully.

The pause enables you to ascertain whether you are acting like a mature adult or like a child. It is quite amazing how often decisions made in childhood limit our resources for coping with stress. By adulthood, most of these childhood decisions are no longer conscious. The same ways of acting have been repeated so many times that we are no longer aware of having ever made a choice. However, unless these childhood choices are changed, they become the rules of the game of our lives. Every need to be met, every problem to be solved has to be handled within these very limited choices made in early childhood.

This has become obvious to me in my therapeutic work as patient after patient says, 'I'm a born worrier. I can't change because *that's the way I am.*' Or 'I've always been like that. I can't help it.' What such patients are saying is that when stresses occur to create a problem, they are unable to cope because of the 'rules' about how they have to act and because of the role they have decided to adopt early in their lives. They are allowing life to control them because of the limited choices they give themselves. They do not permit themselves to think in different ways, therefore they continually create distress for themselves, such distress being reflected in various forms of physical discomfort.

Mental attitude and physical discomfort

The world and those in it do not necessarily cause pain. Nor does our sense of equanimity and peace depend on the conditions of our external environment or on the condition of our body as we perceive it. Rather, each of us is responsible for the world he or she sees and for the feelings he or she experiences. In other words, our thoughts cause the world we experience.

Experience with hypnosis offers some confirmation for this view. Through suggestion and mental imagery it is possible for us to change our sense of time and space, gain relief from pain, alter our state of consciousness, change our perception and affect healing. It is almost as if the mind in the hypnotic state does not accept the conscious definition of what is and is not possible. We can view the mind as if it were a motion picture film, using various techniques to wipe off unwanted old pictures and replacing them with new pictures of ourselves as we want to be. In this way, we are making our own reality.

I do this with many of my own patients. After guiding them into a relaxed state by having them concentrate on their own breathing rhythm, allowing their muscles to 'let go', and their minds to drift, while they contemplate some pleasant, peaceful memory, I suggest they are able to visualize themselves sitting in front of a screen. On this screen they 'see' themselves tossing and turning, unable to get to sleep. They then allow the image to fade, replacing it with one of themselves resting comfortably in bed, sleeping peacefully. When they have this image as they want it, they 'go into' the picture on the screen themselves, experiencing the feelings of restful sleep. Often this very simple procedure means the end of a patient's insomnia.

Or, equally simply, I might invoke the concept of an unconscious mind that can solve problems and promote healing. Let's take insomnia as the difficulty again. Pat

Loadman had suffered from this problem for over ten years. As she enjoyed her pleasant memory, I suggested that her unconscious mind locate something very important from her past life—a time when she slept well, fell asleep easily and enjoyed restful, undisturbed nights, waking in the morning alert and energetic. Pat's unconscious mind would revive this experience in images, sounds and feelings, studying it very, very thoroughly. Through this careful examination, her unconscious mind would learn what was involved in Pat sleeping well and would do everything that was necessary so she could do so in the future.

Probably, this is all lies. There may be no such thing as an unconscious mind. But it works. Pat let go of her insomnia as if it had never existed, so for her it was not a lie but a truth. Using variations of this same method I have helped people lose weight, stop smoking, perform better at sport and in business, gain relief from pain, and get rid of various psychosomatic illnesses. So I believe there is such a thing as an unconscious mind which can help us change in ways we want to change. Maybe we can create our own reality, once we can change our systems of belief and admit that it might be possible.

When we suspend judgement and try out things for ourselves to see if they work for us in achieving the results we want, we certainly have good prospects of 'healing' many of our physical discomforts. We can, for example, achieve considerable pain relief by creating the illusion that mind and body are separate, that we can view *a* body in the bed which may be experiencing pain but it is not *our* body. Similarly, past traumatic events can be visualized in the form of a big, black bird which crashes into the sea and drowns, disappearing completely from our lives.

I will not elaborate further upon the concept of mental healing, for two of my previous books, *The Plus Factor: A Guide to Positive Living* and *The Healing*

Factor: A Guide to Positive Health both discuss it in some detail. They make the point quite strongly that it is advisable to avoid using words like 'limitation, impossible, cannot, try, if only, but, too difficult, ought to', and 'should', for these are words that limit us. They prevent us from finding out that we have incredibly powerful resources within us which enable us to do many things we felt to be 'impossible'.

One of these is to use relaxation as a means of minimizing pain. Pain, of course, serves a very useful function, warning us that something is wrong about which action should be taken. Perhaps we withdraw from a particular situation or keep still so that the injured part is protected. However, some pain outlives its original purpose, becoming very distressful, perhaps leading to exhaustion and depression.

As with any form of stress, individuals differ in the way they react to pain. Some people feel it more readily than others—their threshold, or level at which pain is felt, being quite low. This pain threshold varies not only between people but within individuals at different times. When we are tense, tired, depressed, unwell or apprehensive, we feel pain more than we do when we are caught up in the excitement and eustress of a situation. Sportsmen and women, for example, sometimes suffer quite serious injury of which they are totally unaware until their event is over.

Pain can, in fact, be unnoticed or disappear under many different circumstances. How often a really excruciating toothache vanishes once we are seated in the dentist's waiting room, or a painful stomach ache disappears once the school examination is over! Pain would appear not to be so much an objective reality as a function of something within the person experiencing the pain. If this is so, it means we can learn ways of 'switching off' discomfort. Relaxation is one of the most effective of these.

This is being recognized in hospitals where, for

example, anaesthetists are teaching relaxation techniques to patients who are about to have an operation, so that they will feel less pain afterwards. Also, hospital staff have found that patients who can relax require fewer pain-killing drugs. Dental patients, too, can benefit from relaxation while they are in the waiting room. Such relaxation may be a simple as focusing awareness on the breathing rhythm and letting each out-breath carry tension from body and mind. Then, when the patient is in the dental chair, he or she can concentrate on his or her hands, allowing them to become, loose, floppy and still. By focusing on doing this, and upon breathing calmly, many people are able to greatly reduce the discomfort they would normally experience.

Managing pain, then, is often a matter of letting go. This same approach is, in fact, of great value in managing many forms of stress, so we'll consider the role of relaxation more fully in the next chapter.

6 More on Managing Stress

The value of relaxation

It makes good sense to learn how to relax. As we have seen, relaxing can raise the threshold of pain and often causes aches and pains due to improper muscle tension to completely disappear. In addition, relaxation can help us to avoid unnecessary fatigue, assist recovery from strenuous exercise, improve physical skills through avoidance of unnecessary muscle tension, lower anxiety before a demanding event, and enrich personal relationships since relaxed people are easier to get along with. Generally speaking, it is a most effective way of coping with stress and the disorders it causes.

Just as muscle tension is associated with arousal and anxiety, so relaxation can induce feelings of calm. The key point about relaxing is that it is not really something you do—'I'm going to learn to relax if it's the last thing I do'—but something you do not do. It is a letting go of all effort, something that is easier to do than keeping yourself tense. Yet often the very people who most need to relax are unable to accept the idea that there is something they could do to relieve their distress. Somehow they seem afraid of what might happen if they did 'let go' of their tension.

However, thousands of people can testify to the beneficial results when techniques of relaxation are adopted, particularly in terms of the removal of stress-related discomforts. Insomnia is one of the most prevalent of these and it might be worth considering how the use of relaxation can bring relief to those who suffer from this problem.

Although prolonged insomnia does no permanent damage to mind or body, it does create anxiety in those who find it difficult to get to sleep at night. John Tyson is such a person. Fortunately, John is able to see that it is his own worrying about not getting sufficient sleep that causes his distress rather than the actual insomnia itself. He is also able to accept the idea that if a person remains quiet and calm, with muscles relaxed and mind occupied with pleasant thoughts, he or she obtains probably 80%-90% of the benefits conferred by a good night's sleep.

John's particular method of achieving this relaxed state involves snuggling down in bed, taking two or three calm, slow breaths, accentuating the outbreath and then pausing a moment after each breath is released. Beginning with his eyes open, he gradually lets his eyelids close during the last slow breath. John then feels himself sinking heavily into the bed as he relaxes each part of his body in turn. He always begins at his head and finishes with his toes. Although the actual sequence used does not really matter, it seems to help if a routine is established so that parts of the body are relaxed in the same order each time.

Should John find other thoughts intruding, interfering with his focus on letting go of his muscles, he simply allows them to drift through his mind. He does this by thinking of his mind as a blue sky and each unwanted thought as a small cloud. These drift across the sky and disappear so that the uninterrupted blueness is maintained. Once the cloud has vanished, John returns to focus on his relaxing muscles, 'sending his breath' to any which retain any tension. That is, he breathes in quietly and, as he exhales, imagines the breath going to the tight muscle, soothing it and helping it let go.

Anxiety is the enemy of sleep because it produces the

chemicals in the body which keeps us awake. Through his realization that his relaxation will produce virtually all the benefits of sleep, John has ceased to worry about not sleeping. Because of this, he now invariably drifts off into sleep as he goes through the relaxation routine outlined above. John has also realized that he actually needs less sleep than he thought he did, and this has also helped him turn off the worrying which was the main cause of his insomnia.

For many people, it is really what happens during the day that determines whether they will sleep well at night. Poor sleepers often benefit from one or two short sessions of relaxation, or even a brief nap, in the daytime. Again, it removes some of the anxiety about being awake at night if you know there is a chance to catch up. Generally speaking, inactivity is the precursor of sleep so it is advisable to slow down physical and mental activity as bedtime approaches. Taking a walk or some other exercise before retiring is not a good idea for those with sleeping problems. A warm bath would be more likely to produce the desired result.

Though I have emphasized physical relaxation as an antidote to insomnia, mental relaxation is equally important. There are many ways of achieving this, such as imagining a pleasant scene, letting your mind drift in the direction of a pleasing memory, thinking of a soft, black velvet curtain, or visualizing a lake with the surface of the water unruffled and glassy smooth. Another useful technique is to imagine you are looking at a blackboard. In your hand is an eraser. Every time a thought enters your mind as represented by the blackboard, use the eraser to wipe it clean. If you keep your blackboard clean for about thirty seconds you will usually fall asleep.

This idea may also be used very fruitfully during the day when something stressful happens, causing you to feel tense and anxious. Imagine the blackboard in your mind and write on it, in just a word or two, the cause of your stress. Then wipe these words from the blackboard and out of your mind, seeing only the blackness.

Relaxation of key body areas

Successful relaxation normally involves three aspects. One is mental, such as thinking of blackness. Another is slow, deep breathing, perhaps focusing on the tip of the nose as the breath passes in and out, or upon the abdomen as it rises and falls. The third is muscular relaxation, often seen not only as a means of releasing physical tension but also as a way of controlling thoughts and emotions. This assumption is based on the premise that it is difficult to be emotionally upset if you deliberately let go muscle tension.

Some areas of the body are more important than others as far as physical and emotional relaxation is concerned. When, for example, the *hands* are kept tense, the whole body is geared for action. Therefore, let them relax when they are not involved in the task at hand or when you are under pressure. Another key point is the *brow*. Relax your brow and it is virtually impossible to feel worried. Try this next time you have a problem to solve. Also relax your *jaw* at such times. Whenever you feel hurried, inadequate, doubting of your abilities, or anxious about results, notice what is happening with your jaw. It will probably be clenched tightly shut. Quite possibly, your *abdomen* will also be held tightly, particularly if you are feeling insecure.

To achieve increased relaxation as you go about your daily tasks, check on these four key areas, especially when you feel angry or upset. If you wish, you can deliberately tense them further, then let them relax. By doing this, you remind yourself that it is you who is making your muscles tense and you who can let them go. However, as far as relaxing your jaw is concerned, yawning is probably the best way. Really deep yawning is one of nature's best remedies for tiredness and tension. That is why we often do it during times of stress. Letting the lower jaw drop a little until the mouth is slightly open helps too.

If you keep hands, brow, jaw and abdomen relaxed, you will be able to relieve much of your distress. Should you wish for greater body relaxation than created by letting go of the tension in these areas, you can ease your face by smiling, relax your tongue by placing its tip lightly behind your lower teeth and holding it there without pressure for a while, and rest your eyes by changing focus. If you are concentrating on something at close range, look out of the window at some distant object which is as far away as possible. Quickly shift your gaze back and forth from far to near object, and from a large to a small one, but don't stare.

Should you be suffering from sinus congestion or headache, a further relaxing action you might care to take would be single nostril breathing. Close your right nostril with your thumb, inhaling with your left nostril dilated. Close your left nostril with your forefinger and exhale through your right nostril. Do this rapidly several times, then alternate nostrils. If the pain you are experiencing lies in your neck rather than your head, place your hands so that the fingertips meet at the base of the skull and lift hard, stretching your neck muscles. This you may need to repeat approximately every half hour.

One of the most useful ways of reminding yourself to check on your state of physical relaxation is to watch other people. As you walk along a street, or sit in a bus or train, observe the signs of tension you see around you. These generally show themselves as furrowed brows, contorted faces, clenched jaws and irritability. When you see such signs, use it as a signal to monitor your own situation. Are your jaws clamped tight, your hands clenched and your abdominal muscles held tight? They don't have to be. You are simply burning up energy unnecessarily, holding yourself in a state of readiness for action which is inappropriate—and stressful.

Conversely, if you should have friends or acquaintances who are relaxed, use them as models. Observe them, study them, watch the way they walk and talk, so you can begin acting 'as if' you, too, are a relaxed person. When an actor plays a part, he starts off aware of the separateness between himself and the character he is acting. However, quite quickly, this sense of separation disappears and he becomes the role he is playing. You can do likewise. Play the part of a relaxed person and you will find, quite soon, that you are no longer pretending. Instead you have become the relaxed person you want to be. Another way of achieving this goal is to deliberately set aside specific practice periods each day.

Relaxation training

Virtually all forms of relaxation therapy involve certain principles:
- adopting a relaxing posture
- enjoying a good stretch
- consciously 'letting go' areas of muscle tension
- conjuring up mental pictures of heaviness, warmth and ease
- concentrating the mind through a mental focus
- slow, deep, rhythmical breathing.

If a person wishes to become more calm and tranquil, able to take more control over his or her life, then he or she may be prepared to spend a certain amount of time each day deliberately practising the principles listed above.

There are many ways of combining these, many systems promoting relaxation and mental control, but possibly *transcendental meditation* (TM) is the one most publicized at the present time. This is what made it attractive to Dawn Hazleton, a housewife who experienced tension and anxiety as constant companions.

After two evening lectures, an hour of individual training and a simple initiation ceremony, Dawn, as a new meditator, received her 'mantra'. This short, easily pronounced but essentially meaningless sound she repeated to herself, eyes closed, body relaxed, to achieve a state of conscious restfulness for twenty minutes twice a day. During this twenty-minute period, Dawn simply let her mind wander free, not thinking about anything in particular—although, of course, her mantra did come frequently to mind. If she found herself starting to get too involved in a particular train of thought she would turn it off by focusing on her mantra.

Experimental work suggests that when people meditate in this way, their bodies relax so as to reverse the reactions associated with stress. That is, blood pressure drops, there is an increased level of deep rest, oxygen consumption is reduced, heart rate stabilizes, and production of alpha brain waves increases.

Although Dawn did find her daily sessions of TM helpful in reducing her tension, she stopped her practice after several months. Many people do this, being unwilling to submit themselves to a rather rigid discipline of two twenty-minute periods at set times of the day. Others welcome the discipline and derive great benefits from it. Again, just as perception of stress varies according to the individual, so does the perception of the best way of managing the problem.

One of the objections raised to TM is its spiritual or religious underpinning. Although some people find this quite acceptable, others say it interferes with their acceptance of it as a means of reducing their stress level. Accordingly, when Herbert Benson, in his book, *The Relaxation Response*, pointed out that all the benefits of TM could be gained without the necessity of embracing any of the religious aspects, his ideas were very popular. He suggested that a person practise in the following way at any time with the proviso that he or she does not do so within the two hours after a meal:

- in an area as free of distractions as possible, assume a comfortable sitting position with no undue muscle tension
- have eyes closed
- deeply relax all muscles
- breathe through nose—as you breathe out, say 'one' to yourself. If distracting thoughts occur, let them pass through and return to 'one'
- practise for 10–20 minutes. When finished, sit quietly with eyes closed, then with eyes open
- adopt a passive 'let-it-happen' attitude, permitting relaxation to occur at its own pace.

Benson's 'relaxation response' does seem to work well for a lot of people in that they are able to carry over the benefits of the practise sessions into their everyday lives, becoming increasingly unruffled by things which would previously have created tension.

Others seem to prefer variants of Benson's technique, using the floor, for example, instead of a chair. In fact, Dawn Hazleton, referred to earlier in relation to her practice of TM, found the following approach one she was able to use every day with beneficial results. Lying on the floor with rolled-up towels under her neck, small of back and knees, she takes a deep breath and tenses the body, doing this three or four times. As she lets her breath go the last time, she feels her body sinking into the floor. After enjoying this sensation for a minute or two, she focuses on her feet, feels them relax, and imagines a comfortable feeling like warm oil flowing up her legs into her body, shoulders, arms, hands, fingers, neck and face. As the 'oil' reaches her eyes, she rolls them gently back, and 'sees' in her mind the flow of breath as it comes and goes rhythmically in and out of her nostrils. Usually the rhythm becomes slower and slower, deeper and deeper, as Dawn lets go all tension. Often she meditates quite spontaneously at this time, something she describes as 'taking a holiday in her head' which she finds very refreshing. Superficially, this technique of Dawn's seems very little different from that of TM which she tried and rejected. Yet obviously she finds the approach just described fits her needs whereas the TM approach did not. As always, it is a matter of trying things out to find what produces the results you want.

A simple return to nature, for instance, may provide the relaxation you seek just as well, or better, than the relaxation practice described in this section. For one thing, when we contemplate the vastness and mystery of the universe, it is difficult for us to exaggerate the trivial pressures of our own lives. We get a healthy sense of perspective, becoming aware of our tendency to turn molehills into mountains. Also, getting in touch with nature induces a sense of timelessness, a spirit of tranquillity which is markedly at odds with our own desperate haste to get things done. Nature will not be hurried. The tides ebb and flow in their own rhythm, the sun rises and sets irrespective of human desires, and seasons follow each other in their regular orderly pattern.

Nature has, too, a sense of permanence, unity and harmony, a feeling of simplicity and dependability. That is why we can find relief from distress through the occasional return to a simpler way of life more closely attuned to our agricultural origins. Walks in the country, or by the sea, camping, bird-watching and gardening are all ways of re-experiencing a kinship with nature which is calming, and which provides a sense of renewal. Such activities also provide exercise, a most important antidote to stress.

The importance of exercise

Sometimes people unknowingly discover how to release their tension. When upset or worried they turn to some activity that uses many of the large muscles of the body. Strenuous gardening, window cleaning or running around the block are all activities that usually make us feel better. This is because we are tensing our muscles to some purpose and so preventing the accumulation of the stress chemicals in our bodies.

Sport is often called relaxation because it provides an opportunity for us to channel our tense, aggressive feelings on to a ball or a muscular activity. Sport allows us to vent our anger in socially acceptable ways. After all, hitting a tennis or squash ball is a good alternative to hitting your boss or the parking meter attendant.

Of course, a lot depends on the sport you choose. If you are playing sport to relax, playing in competition with others may not be a good idea as tension is usually raised by such activity. Even playing in competition with yourself, as in a sport such as golf, can be rather counter-productive. There seems little point in finishing a game, whatever it might be, more tense and distressed than when you started. On the other hand, competitive sport is ideally suited for those who seek to achieve success and personal satisfaction in some sphere outside their daily work.

Exercise assists us to cope with stress in many ways. As already pointed out, it provides a means of 'letting off steam' which is approved of by society. It also reduces our anxiety level by speeding up the rate at which lactic acid is oxidized and removed from circulation. Stamina is increased, too, enabling us to cope more effectively with the demands of the environment. Exercise counteracts the biochemical effects of stress, a factor of great importance if we accept Carruthers' claim in *The Western Way of Death* that the combination of a high level of emotional activity with a low level of physical activity deranges body chemistry and is the major cause of heart disease. Exercise, in fact, would seem to reduce the risk of illness generally, particularly psychological illness, for a close correlation between mental health and physical fitness does seem to exist.

People who do not exercise allow their bodies to become incapable of coping with an extra strain or effort. Our hearts can function reasonably well, for instance, as long as our existence is undemanding. However, should we have to run hard for a bus we may find ourselves in trouble. It seems that the human body thrives on hard work, becoming stronger the more it is used. This is borne out by a study of United Kingdom civil servants. Of those who exercised regularly, 11% had heart disease. This compared favourably with the non-exercisers who had a 26% heart disease rate. The authors of the study suggested swimming, tennis, hill climbing, dancing, digging, running and tree felling as particularly effective forms of exercise.

Short periods of regular exercise, as little as fifteen minutes two or three times a week, can be very helpful in improving the function of heart, muscles and circulatory system. Stamina increases as a result, so that a dash for a bus or a climb up several flights of stairs becomes less of a stressful ordeal.

Should you wish to, you can test your heart's ability to cope with extra stresses and strains. Find a step with a 30 cm (12") drop or use a low stool or bench. For each of three minutes, step up 24 times, which is the equivalent of ascending and descending 72 steps. Each step involves stepping up with the right foot, moving left foot alongside the right, stepping down with the right foot, and then stepping down with the left foot. When you have completed the exercise, sit down, wait for five seconds, then measure your pulse beat during the following minute. If it is below 80, you are very fit. Average fitness lies in the 80-100 range, and unfitness is the interpretation if your heart rate is over 100. Should the rate be over 130 beats a minute, you are in really poor condition.

An alternative way of measuring your fitness is to note the amount of time you take to cover a fixed distance, either running or walking. If you are unable to cover a mile in 12 minutes, your fitness leaves much to be desired. Should you wish to improve matters, remember to do so slowly. The simplest type of exercise is walking, yet it is one which is very beneficial to virtually every muscle in the body. Perhaps that is why dog owners who regularly exercise their pets tend to be reasonably fit. Even when they are not very keen on getting out, the feel they owe it to their dogs.

They may get an extra bonus, too, for it has been claimed that pet owners generally have lower blood pressure than non-pet owners, partly due to the additional exercise but also partly due to the relaxing effect of stroking and patting. Apparently, expressing affection in this way is good for both pet and owner and it does seem a nice way to reduce stress levels. Perhaps we should pat and stroke our spouses, boy and girl friends more often. Not only would it make them, and us, feel better, it might also help us turn off the stress of work.

Managing work stress

To work without fatigue, it is necessary to adopt a rhythm of alternate periods of activity and rest. *Resting before we actually become tired* is a good idea, one practised by Rosalie Benson, a shop assistant of my acquaintance. During her coffee and lunch breaks, or whenever she has a lull in customers wanting attention, she spends two to three minutes in passive relaxation. Whenever possible she sits down, giving her whole weight to the chair, the weight of her legs and feet to the floor, and allows herself to increasingly 'melt' into the chair as she counts each breath that she lets go.

Taking a break in this way reduces Rosalie's tension, increases her energy and seems to speed up her reaction time. After all, animals sleep at irregular intervals during the day when they are tired. It is only we humans who have imposed the custom of limiting our rest to the hours of darkness. Not all of us, of course. Afternoon siestas are still popular in many countries. However, if we cannot create the conditions to allow us to have a nap during our lunch break, we can still derive a lot of benefit from momentary relaxation pauses.

This is because, as we work, we tense muscles unnecessarily. Look at any office. Notice how many people are hunched over their desks, eyes screwed up, brows furrowed, teeth clenched and legs held under their chairs. Brief breaks, which allow muscles to let go, eyes to close or focus on a pleasant scene outside the window, and minds to drift into pleasant memories, relieve this tension and also improve work efficiency.

Remember, it is not necessary to lie down to relax. You can practise in the bus, in an office chair or under the hair drier. Also, remember that relaxation can be as refreshing as sleep—sometimes more so, for many people spend a lot of time tossing, turning and gritting their teeth while enjoying the supposed blessed release of sleep. Even breathing slowly and calmly two or three times when faced with a demanding situation can be immensely valuable in reducing your stress level.

So, too, can a little *self-massage*. Smooth gently out from the centre of the forehead towards the temples, and then upwards towards the hair line, one hand after another. This is a great help for tired eyes, headaches and the general feeling of being under strain. Using your finger tips to find tender spots on your neck and shoulders, and to then press and let go with circular movements without stretching the skin can be of assistance, too. Perhaps, even more valuable is the foot massage I have described in *The Healing Factor*. Probing the feet to find sensitive spots and massaging them until the sensitivity decreases and disappears can be most beneficial in releasing tension.

Stress on the job can be handled in other ways. When change is necessary, plan it together with everyone who is going to be involved in it. Sometimes this is not possible, but every effort should be made to include as many as possible of the people to be affected. Maintaining continued contact with colleagues, particularly subordinates, makes for a less stressful atmosphere—limits of tasks may be defined and support given to accomplishment. It is really a matter of ensuring a free flow of communication, of providing opportunities for people to talk over work matters on a daily basis if they want to do so.

Getting along with other people, which is usually helped by open lines of communication, usually reduces stress on the job considerably. This is particularly true when the other person is your boss. Probably the single thing which can most effectively facilitate good relationships between you is to help the person feel important, to enhance a sense of adequacy. How this might be achieved is outlined in the chapter on managing other people, but the basic strategy is to provide 'strokes', perhaps in the form of positive comments on things done well. It is particularly important to be encouraging and supportive when the boss is going through something now labelled 'the mid-life crisis'.

This label refers to people who feel their careers and entire lives have reached some sort of a plateau. There is no excitement any more, no opportunities for major satisfaction, only a rather painful acceptance that they have probably gone as far as they are going to go, that they will never achieve some long-standing and cherished ambitions.

Peter Ferguson, an executive employed by a chain of kitchenware retailers, was 48 years old when he found himself deep in his mid-life crisis. It had crept up on him, virtually unnoticed, and for some time he drifted with no sense of direction. Lacking energy, seeing his road to further promotion blocked, and feeling too old to start again in another firm, Peter was revealing the usual symptoms of distress, becoming increasingly irritable and impatient, complaining of head and stomach aches, and sleeping badly. The mid-life crisis is a very stressful experience, one that can bring with it illness and unhappiness.

Fortunately for Peter, his older brother Lance had successfully survived his own mid-life crisis several years earlier and was able to give him the benefit of his experience. He suggested to Peter that he take a hard look at the goals he had set himself, liberating himself from those desires he now knew he could not satisfy, and establishing personal targets which he identified as being of prime importance. It is easy, Lance pointed out, to unquestioningly accept as your own the goals of others and to travel at the pace others set for you. Peter needed little convincing on this score, because one of his best friends, whose main target was to organize his work so he could spend more time with his family, had just accepted a promotion which meant he had less time to do what he really wanted. Peter could see the frustration and stress created by this conflict.

Another of Peter's friends had amassed a considerable fortune. He had far more money than he needed, yet he continually drove himself to create more wealth. There would be no problem with this if he was happy doing so, but he was not. The more money he made, the more possessions he acquired, the more he worried about losing what he had acquired. The Tahitian proverb, 'A man who has a big canoe has big problems' fitted this man very well and Peter saw the havoc being wreaked on his health through his pursuit of conflicting goals.

Peter agreed with Lance. He would set his personal targets and adopt his own pace to achieve them. This meant he would modify his frenetic striving, working steadily and efficiently, but not so hard that his performance would deteriorate under excessive strain. Further, if he failed in one approach, he would be sufficiently flexible to try something else for, as the Zen Buddhists have it, 'The journey is more important than the destination.' The old adage 'If at first you don't succeed, try, try and try again', which Peter had observed rather rigidly, he now relinquished in favour of a more flexible guideline, 'If at first you don't succeed, try something different.'

Though it took time, and though he was rarely 100% successful, Peter was able to take stock of his life and to make the sort of changes indicated above. By doing so, he took a lot of pressure off himself and the symptoms of stress gradually disappeared. He does his job as capably as ever, but without pushing so hard. In fact, because he is now more relaxed, he gets on better with colleagues and customers alike.

Peter seems to be making better decisions, too. He has reduced the strain of decision making by taking it in an orderly fashion, first making a detailed statement of the problem, formulating all the solutions he can think of, evaluating these solutions and selecting the best solution. Sometimes he takes the last step consciously, but more frequently he makes use of the unconscious problem-solving method I have explained in *The Plus Factor*. Once he has assembled all the relevant information he hands the probem over to his unconscious mind and refuses to think consciously about it for several days. If no answer has come to him by that time, he again reviews the available information and waits. Normally, the solution arrives while Peter is showering, playing golf or reading a novel. He fervently believes that decisions arrived at in this way are superior to those he has made using only conscious sources of information.

On minor decisions—and if we are truthful, these are the vast bulk of decisions we have to make—he might even use a pendulum as I have described in both *The Plus Factor* and *The Healing Factor*. By allowing the pendulum, which is possibly drawing on unconscious sources of knowledge, to indicate 'yes' or 'no', Peter cuts through the indecisiveness most of us display when having to make up our minds about anything. Like infantry officers who are trained to take firm, courageous action, even at the risk of making occasional mistakes, Peter believes that 'to do the right thing is commendable, to do the wrong thing is regrettable, to do nothing is unforgivable'. Also, once his decision is made, consciously, unconsciously, or through use of the pendulum, Peter lets it go without post-mortems. He learns from his decisions but does not permit them to become the source of constant self-reproach and stress that they were earlier in his life.

Not for Peter the two main traps of the mid-life crisis, because he had experienced them both previously. A few years earlier, he had become the classic workaholic, equating hard work with personal worth. Every failure, every criticism was met by working longer hours, productivity being confused with being busy to such an extent that he perceived any leisure as a waste of time. Hard work would solve all his problems, Peter thought. It didn't. As he recast his goals in mid-life, he realized this. Accordingly, he moderated both the amount of work he did and the time spent working. Rarely did he take home the bulging briefcase of yore. Weekends and evenings he spent with his family—without any noticeable drop in his effectiveness.

Peter also escaped from the guilt trap, the belief that 'I am the one at fault for all my problems'. This is often linked to the workaholic approach. By keeping very busy we can assuage our guilt—we are really doing something. Unfortunately, anger is turned inwards, thus paralysing constructive activity towards coping with stress.

Peter let go the guilt and the workaholic activity. Unfortunately, many people experiencing the mid-life crisis embrace these traps as ways of improving matters. They don't. They only increase stress and the unpleasant symptoms associated with stress. In fact, managing work tension successfully may be more a matter of avoiding overwork. To do this effectively, we need to consider how we use our time.

Time management to minimize stress

Time means clocks, and avoidance of habitual clock-watching is the first step to minimizing time-linked stress. Generally, watching the clock does not help us perform any better but it certainly increases our level of tension. Your car has a flat battery. As you wait for the garage mechanic you constantly look at your watch, fuming and fretting over being late for an appointment. The unhappy glances at your watch do not make one iota of difference to the time you will actually arrive for your appointment. All they do is distress you. That is why the idea of putting a small white dot in the centre of your watch crystal can be so useful in providing a signal for you to slow down, breath deeply, let go the muscles. As the Orientals say, 'Don't push the river, let it flow.' What seems so vital now will be forgotten in a few days.

Working at your own pace, as Peter Ferguson found, is also a good way of managing stress. It is interesting that Peter found he could improve his performance and reduce tension by deliberately slowing down whenever he felt pressurised. Acting in this way, Peter was emulating Albert Tangera, former world champion typist, who would practise for two weeks at about half his best speed whenever he seemed stalled at a particular plateau of typing speed. That is, instead of striving to go faster, he forced himself to practise slowly, a procedure which apparently permitted his unconscious mind to learn to type better. So Peter, whenever he feels hurried, deliberately slows down his physical movements. This nullifies his desire to go faster than his most efficient pace. It is, I suggest, an idea well worth your trying.

So, too, is the procedure of deliberately planning how you will allocate your time. This involves setting realistic goals, working steadily towards their achievement, and prescribing definite starting and finishing dates for your activities. Many experts on time management believe the establishment of goals to be the key to successful living. They would suggest you focus on one objective at a time, always having the next one ready at the back of your mind, because most satisfaction in life comes from pursuing a goal, not simply from achieving it. You could even write your goal on a card and carry it with you, thinking about it every day and creating concrete mental images as if you have already accomplished it. Keeping active in pursuit of goals is, for many people, a way of stimulating themselves to perform at their optimum level, generating eustress. It is only when such activity is overdone, when eustress becomes distress, that it becomes necessary to slow down and reduce arousal.

For goal-setting can be obsessive in that we feel we must always be doing something constructive with our time. Yet, we also need space to enjoy just being, playing and day dreaming. As Ogden Nash expressed it, 'Most people suffer from hardening of the oughteries.' By doing what we feel 'ought' to do, what we 'should' do, we generate internal conflict because, inside, we really do not want to be doing these things. Someone asks you, for instance, to give up your Saturday morning to drive some children to a school activity. To be agreeable, you say 'yes'. You feel you 'ought' to do it but you don't want to, and there is a lot of resentment inside you. To minimize this distress, you need to learn how to say 'no' occasionally, or perhaps more than occasionally, so you can focus on your own goals rather than on those other people provide for you.

Sometimes we are unsure of what is important to us. One way of overcoming this is to write down the three things we want most at present. Keep this list, put it away, and repeat the exercise next week, and for the following six weeks. At the end of this time, take out your eight lists, and look at what you have written.

You'll soon ascertain what is really important to you. It is towards these goals that you should work if you want to minimize distress and maximize eustress. Also, it is a good idea to repeat this listing process about every six months. Our desires change over time and it is easy to continue devoting a lot of time to the pursuit of goals which are no longer important to us.

Providing breathing spaces in each day's schedule helps to reduce pressure. Don't allow work to expand to fill the available space, something that frequently happens with meetings which drag on endlessly even when nothing is being accomplished. Plan breaks for thinking, for it is easy to occupy our time so fully with 'busy-work' that we leave no time to get our lives into perspective, to decide whether we are using our time in the best way. Obviously, in an emergency, this uncommitted time can be used to complete work which has been unavoidably delayed. Simply having this 'reserve space' available is a great anti-distress device whereas the fully committed schedule which leaves no room for manoeuvre is a sure way to increase tension.

What this really means is that it is of great value to keep schedules flexible. Do not create a strait-jacket for yourself. Be prepared to work longer or shorter days as occasion demands, but always ensure that what you are doing needs doing, for this helps you enjoy each day more fully. For many years I accepted intellectually the wisdom of living in 'day-tight compartments', one day at a time, but it took me years before I was able to actually practise this philosophy. We inflict much unnecessary strain on ourselves when we concern ourselves with the failures of the past and the projected disasters of the future. The problems of the present are enough at any one time. It requires little strain to live life minute by minute, because what you are doing is reducing your area of effort to the present moment.

Putting this principle into practice means breaking your work up into small parts, coping with each in order of priority whenever possible. Completion of each part becomes a sub-goal, accomplishment of which gives you a sense of achievement. In fact, being content to do only the small part of the task you have set yourself, rather than hurriedly tackling it in its entirety, helps you work against the Type A personality syndrome of 'I must do it all now'. If we leave some things to be done tomorrow we are likely to greatly increase our chances of living to do them. Remember, you can only do one job at a time so give your whole mind to it without worrying about other things which have to be done. Such worry only uses up vast amounts of energy which could be used in more productive ways. This direction of your energy into those channels likely to produce eustress instead of distress is the essence of any strategy you may use to successfully manage stress. One such strategy involves the concept of playing the *Inner Game*.

7 Stress and the Inner Game

What is the inner game?

Graeme Dickson is a very successful businessman. His associates and his competitors all agree on that. Why? What is it about Graeme that stamps him as special? For one thing, he commands an impressively large salary. For another, other companies are continually trying to entice him into their employment. Further, Graeme has won many awards within his industry and from the Chamber of Commerce on a broader basis. He is much in demand as a guest speaker, one who is able to show others how to better their own performance.

An observer studying Graeme would see more than these 'prizes' he has achieved. He or she would notice his skill in handling people, the clarity of his communication, the effectiveness with which he conducts meetings, solves problems, makes decisions and uses his time. Yes, Graeme plays what I would call the *Outer Game* very well indeed. Less obviously, he also excels in the *Inner Game*.

All of us play the Inner Game. Some play it well, others play it badly. Some of us know we're playing, others have no idea they are even in a contest. What, then, is this Inner Game? As Tim Gallwey has described it in the *Inner Game of Tennis* and *Inner Tennis*, it involves a struggle against internal mental and emotional obstacles for the goal of self-realization. Taking tennis as an example, we all play two games. One of these, the Outer Game, is played against obstacles presented by an external opponent in order to win external prizes. The other is played against the obstacles we create in our own minds which prevent us being the player we are capable of being. This is, of course, true not only for tennis but for life itself.

Every human activity has its external and its internal distress-producing obstacles. The former come from many different sources but the latter come from one source only—the mind, which is so easily distracted and disturbed by its tendency to worry and agonize. Often we develop an upset mind through regretting our past behaviour, or through fear of the future or dislike of a present situation. Yet, it is important to realize that the actual event 'causing' our unhappiness and our reaction to this event are two different things. It is not usually the external event which causes worry and distress but the way in which we choose to react to this event.

The tennis player who misses a couple of shots begins by berating himself for his errors but, once started on this self-blaming train of thought, may quite quickly become so despondent that he begins to doubt his value as a person. Sounds ridiculous, really, yet we do this all the time. Some trivial event occurs, and we make a catastrophe of it, blowing it up out of all proportion to its actual importance. By so doing, we create great distress for ourselves. Yet, by understanding what the Inner Game is all about we can overcome the mental opponent who is causing this disturbance.

To do so, we need to back off a little, to observe ourselves and our reactions, to stay uninvolved. By acting in this way, we come to realize that the problem is more in our mind than in the external events which we believe are causing the upset. That is where the pressure comes from, our imagined beliefs concerning the harmful effects of some particular event.

You really have only two choices in dealing with circumstances which upset you. Either you change those circumstances or you change the attitude of your mind to those circumstances. Therefore, if you are unable to change the situation, you either continue to feel miserable, angry, frustrated—or you decide on a different reaction which will, in turn, help you feel happier.

To illustrate, you arrange to meet a friend for lunch. He's late. You fume, feeling annoyed and frustrated. But you don't have to react in this way. Assuming you still want your lunch and do not intend to leave, you can look upon this event as providing an opportunity for you to play the Inner Game. Your opponent is the negative reaction, the feeling of upset and anger, the thoughts which are adversely affecting you. You can 'win' over your opponent by realizing how unimportant the event actually is. What does it really matter if you sit waiting for a quarter or half-an-hour? Practise changing your thinking, watching the unhappiness-producing thoughts drift through your mind and replacing them with pleasant memories, plans for the future or enjoyment of the present fact that you are alive, well, anticipating a good lunch. Either you control your thoughts and your reactions to events, or they control you. If you allow the latter to happen, you are at the mercy of everything and everyone that comes along. Life runs you instead of you running your life.

With an approach such as I have suggested above, you will find your attitude to the inevitable difficulties of life changes dramatically. Instead of seeing them as enemies, making your life miserable, you can see them as friends, providing opportunities for your growth as a human being. As Gallwey has pointed out, you should love your tennis opponent for he gives you the chance to realize your own potential, to find out just what you are capable of. Similarly, the problems you encounter in your life can be 'loved' in the same way.

To play the Inner Game successfully, it is first necessary to understand the idea. This is a step in the right direction because it involves a change of attitude, this provides the key to any self-improvement. We are normally too prone to ask 'What is making me unhappy?' rather than the more useful 'What am I doing to make myself unhappy?' The latter question shows that you take personal responsibility for your mental state instead of blaming it on others. If you really believe that other people and external circumstances are the cause of your troubles, you are unlikely to improve the quality of your life. However, once you accept that you yourself create most of your own difficulties, you can take steps to remove them. As *you* have placed the obstacles in your mind, *you* are equally able to get rid of them.

The obstacles we create

What are these obstacles we put in our own minds? Fear is one. Joanne Summerhill is a very capable lady, one who has achieved a good position with a Health Benefits fund. However, despite the obvious trappings of her success she has a powerful fear of failure, a fear which often paralyses her and prevents her from making suggestions or taking action in situations where there is a possibility she might be wrong. Joanne is frightened of what people might think or say if she suggests some action which does not work. Though a fear such as this has its roots in her past, perhaps through childhood experiences with parents and teachers, it is Joanne herself who is keeping this fear alive and well now. It is she who, by dwelling on her thoughts of 'Wouldn't it be terrible if I were wrong', is limiting herself. In other words, she is allowing her inner opponent, her fear, to defeat her and make her a less successful person than she would otherwise be.

With fear is often associated a second obstacle—doubt. This may take the form of doubting one's own ability. Joanne has this problem. Despite her achievements, she still has lingering doubts about her ability. Is she really good enough to hold the position she does? Because of this doubt, she fears to offer suggestions in case she might be wrong, and people would then know she was not good enough. This behaviour upsets her, causing her considerable distress, but she seems to be unable to change it.

Unfortunately, this fear–doubt obstacle can be easily magnified to the extent that a person questions his or her value as a human being. If a little thing such as a couple of missed shots at tennis can be magnified in this way, how much easier it is to 'blow up' difficulties in communication as indications of one's failure as a person. The mind has great power as an amplifier or a damper. If we focus on the pain of a headache, we make it worse through the very power of our concentration upon it. Conversely, by deliberately distracting our thoughts away from the headache, by focusing on something else, we diminish the pain. Similarly, by concentrating upon our fears and our doubts we enlarge upon them, creating obstacles in our minds which defeat our efforts to overcome the stress produced by our 'inner' opponents.

Anxiety, worry, tension, call it what you will, is another largely self-imposed obstacle. Ron Williams is a worrier. Even when things are going well he still worries. He actually finds something to become concerned about. One morning Ron passed his boss Bob Grant on the way to his office. Under such conditions, Bob would usually smile and exchange a few words. On this occasion he did not do so, hurrying by in a rather preoccupied manner. For the rest of the morning, Ron wondered what he had done to incur his boss' displeasure. He dredged up every likely and unlikely possibility, fretting about each one, and, of course, getting nothing useful done as far as his work was concerned. His anxiety about being called to Bob's office for a reprimand became so strong that he was unable to concentrate upon anything else. Later, at lunch, he heard from a friend that Bob's father had died the night before and he was very upset about it.

Ron created his own stress. By worrying about someone else's action he set up an obstacle in his own mind which prevented him doing his normal work. We do it all the time, reading our own interpretations into neutral events, accepting these interpretations as real, and proceeding to worry because this 'reality' is threatening to us.

In *Frogs into Princes*, Richard Bandler and John Grinder point out how we each make a 'map of the territory'. On a map, we may represent a river as a thin blue line, a forest as a patch of green, a hospital as a cross. These symbols, the blue line, the patch of green, the cross, are not, however, a river, a forest or a hospital. They only represent or 'stand for' those objects. Similarly, as we grow up, we make a map in our mind of the way the world is. We abstract from our experience a view of reality, and we act in accordance with that view. Unfortunately, we are very prone to forget that is is only *our* interpretation of reality. That is, our map 'stands for' the real world, but it is not the real world.

Ron's map represented his boss' silence as evidence of displeasure. He then proceeded to act as if this representation was true. Perhaps it might have been but, even if this had been so, all Ron accomplished was to waste a morning worrying and feeling tense. As it turned out, his representation was wrong—which made his morning even more of a wasted effort.

Our maps also include another important obstacle which interferes with us playing a winning Inner Game. This is guilt. Engendering guilt in someone is a marvellous way of controlling that person's behaviour. Our parents knew that. So did our teachers. Accordingly, we still carry in our minds many guilts placed there while we were too young to realize what was happening. As adults we do not have to let these remain, we do not have to allow them to still exercise any control over our behaviour. Yet we do, just as we allow our colleagues, competitors, spouses and children to manipulate us through the guilt feelings they arouse.

Jan Stirling wanted to return to work. Before the birth of her first child, she was a talented graphic artist working in an advertising agency. As her children grew up, Jan was a full-time mother. Now, with her children both at work, she wanted to do more than look after her house and her husband, Don. Don, however, was not happy with the idea of Jan going to work. He liked having her at home, a support system ready to be called on whenever it was convenient for him. So Don pointed out that by going back to work Jan would be depriving a school leaver of a job. Through her selfishness, she would be taking money which she really did not need from someone who needed it desperately. Knowing Jan's strong social conscience and her concern for unemployment among school leavers, Don played on her guilt feelings.

However, Don can only be successful if Jan co-operates with him by feeling guilty. That is, she is the one who must create the obstacle which prevents her doing what she feels is right for her and employing her unused abilities as a graphic artist. Don cannot create the obstacle if Jan refuses to accept his thoughts as relevant to her. That is what playing the Inner Game successfully is all about. The limitations preventing you being the person you are capable of being are largely self-created. After all, it is *your* 'map of the territory'. If the map you have is full of limitations, of obstacles saying 'you cannot do this', 'you're not good enough to do that', then change your map.

The skills of the Inner Game

In his books Gallwey describes several skills which equip a person to be a good Inner Game player. The first of these is *concentration*, the ability to focus the mind on something of your choice. Normally, our mind drifts, a prey to random thoughts and environmental influences. Yet, unless we control our mind by providing a focus for concentration, it controls us.

It is amazing how often a random thought, a comment made by a colleague, a word read in a report, can start us off on a quite self-destructive tack in which trivialities are magnified out of all proportion to their lack of worth. When such things occur, deliberately switch your mind away to something else upon which you can concentrate. It might be some work, your own breathing rhythm, an object on your desk which pleases you, a sound or word which you can use as an inner focus. You might focus on the actual movement of your hand, the pull of muscles in your arm as you pick up the phone. Feal the texture of the receiver, its pressure against your ear. Experience the contact of your finger against the dial. By concentrating in this way, you interrupt the disturbing influence and take control of your attention.

Actually, this interrupting is a way to create a new habit. Many people say 'I can't stop thinking about . . .' whatever it is that is worrying them. They act as if some external force was making them think in this distressful way. Surely we have the power to decide what we are going to think about. We exercise this power by deliberately interrupting unwanted thoughts and turning our attention to something else which we have chosen as worthy of our attention. As we practise such interruption, it becomes a habit, so that unwanted thoughts tend to trigger, automatically, the shift of attention.

Habits do not arise by themselves, of course. Concentration needs practice. Personally, I find it very valuable to use 'waiting time' to practise. We spend considerable time each week in waiting for somebody, or for something to happen. On such occasions we may fret or fume, or sit quietly thinking of nothing in particular. Yet, if we want to, we can make this time when we are waiting for people, such as doctors, dentists, colleagues and spouses, or for objects such as public transport, serve a very valuable function.

Consider this situation. You have an appointment with your doctor. He is delayed due to his involvement in an emergency operation. Decide you will use this unexpected free time profitably. Focus on your thoughts. Watch them streaming into and through your mind. Let them drift away until one comes along which you want to explore further. Concentrate on this and, if you find your attention wandering to something else, firmly bring it back to the thought you have selected.

Or perhaps you would prefer simply to choose a word, for example 'power' and investigate it more fully. Concentrate on this word and its meaning for you until you seem to have exhausted its possibilities. Then, think of several words at random, words such as 'water', 'wife' and 'coffee'. Now, explore possible connections between 'power' and 'water'. When you have gone as far as you can, do the same for 'power' and 'wife', and then 'power' and 'coffee'. All sorts of fascinating ideas are generated as you concentrate in this way. Not only do you practise a valuable skill, you will often develop interesting ideas to try out in your life. An added bonus is that time passes very quickly and you release yourself from the tension so often associated with waiting.

A second useful skill which it helps Inner Game players to acquire is that of *suspension of judgement*. This simply means that you see things as they are instead of adding to them. The tennis player hits the ball into the net and tells himself he is useless. The housewife forgets to buy some meat and berates herself for being incompetent. In each case there is an event, a stroke into the net, a forgotten purchase and a judgment on that event—'I'm useless', 'I'm incompetent'.

Events are neutral. They are neither good nor bad, but thinking makes them so. It is our reaction to events, our judgement, which adds the emotional element. Perhaps our parents, teachers, church leaders and community elders have told us that we should evaluate our actions, blaming ourselves for mistakes (though they are less happy about us congratulating ourselves for the good things we do) and generally resolving to do better. But does this help?

Consciously willing ourselves to play a better tennis shot next time usually results in tight muscles and an anxious mind which virtually ensures another error. Similarly, consciously willing ourselves to exert more effort in remembering what we have to buy often leads to a tension and strain which saps our effectiveness. Not always, of course. Sometimes we can achieve improvement through will-power but, more often, the subconscious conditioning technique explained in the chapter on reprogramming the mind is likely to be more useful. As this programming takes effect, we just let things happen and observe them.

Letting things happen without interference from the conscious mind is a third skill of the Inner Game player. Whereas the unsuccessful player of this game is constantly judging his performance, putting the labels of 'good', 'bad', 'terrible', 'fantastic' on everything he does, the successful player coolly observes his actions and mentally records the results.

Not for him the agonizing self-blame over the netted tennis shot. Instead he observes that he hit the ball too early so it went into the net. No judgment here, no self-condemnation for being a useless tennis player; instead, a detached self-observation, a noting of the event which occurred.

The housewife observes her actions in doing the family shopping. She does what seems appropriate. However, she forgets something. Self-recrimination will not help. Instead, she records what happened and next time, tries something different, such as making a better list of necessary purchases. This attitude of just letting things happen without too much conscious guidance is the secret of success in most ventures. If something does not work, do not waste time blaming yourself, try something else instead and note the results. Keep doing so until you gain the outcome you want. Your actions are not 'good' or 'bad'. They either produce the desired results or they do not. It is the outcome which is important, not the judgmental label.

A fourth skill is important here. When some action does not produce the desired outcome, when some event, neutral though it may be, results in dissatisfaction, our usual response is anger and frustration. We become annoyed because things have not worked out the way we wanted them to. Yet, we can adopt another attitude under such circumstances, one likely to produce better results. We can *welcome failures* because they give us the opportunities for growth and development. This way we cannot lose. If things are going smoothly, we can enjoy our good fortune; if failures or difficulties arise, we can enjoy the opportunities for growth.

The successful Inner Game player cannot lose. External obstacles are observed without judgment. The player concentrates on what is happening, mentally records the events which are occurring without adding his own emotional reactions, decides on appropriate action and lets it all happen. Should he fail to achieve the results he desires, he wastes no time in self-blame but tries different actions, noting their outcomes, until he is successful.

8 Winning the Inner Game

Self observation

In the previous chapter I referred to the successful Inner Game player as one who coolly watches his own behaviour, noting the results he achieves in a rather detached manner. This is the essence of self-observation. It is as if we divide ourselves into two, an outer personality and an inner 'I' or 'eye'. The outer personality goes through its normal actions, plays its normal roles, while the inner 'I' watches it doing so.

Such self-observation is the condition necessary if we are to change ourselves. Until we become aware of our behaviour, our thoughts, our feelings, our contra-dictions, we are full of 'dark places' which prevent us taking more control over our stress level. This is because we simply do not know what we are like. Observation lets light into these 'dark places' helping us see things about ourselves, the existence of which we did not even suspect. Armed with this new awareness, we can then attempt to change ourselves, should we so desire. We may be unsuccessful in our attempts, of course, but without self-observation we have no hope at all.

Consider Leon James. A very successful real estate salesman, Leon is much concerned with ethics. He serves on a number of committees whose aim is to prepare a code of ethics for the 'profession', and often speaks at functions on the importance of integrity and honesty in business activities. In similar vein, he exhorts his children to accept that honesty is always the best policy. Yet, many associates and customers see him as a 'crook'. To them, his sharp practices in selling real estate either border on the dishonest or are actually illegal. Leon loses no opportunity to clinch a sale, even if this involves outright lying and betrayal of the seller's best interests.

Leon is quite unaware of this contradiction in his behaviour. It is as if there is a barrier in his mind, separating his belief in his honesty from his dishonest behaviour. This is what I mean by 'dark places'. He simply does not see that he is dishonest and, should it be suggested to him that his behaviour leaves much to be desired ethically, he would not believe it. However, he is very quick to point the accusatory finger at any other real estate salesman who he feels is acting unethically.

This ability to see a fault in others which we fail to see in ourselves is a very common human attribute, one which Freud labelled projection. There are things about ourselves which, if we faced them, we would not like. Therefore, instead of facing them we project them outwards, identifying them in other people whom we can then dislike for possessing such unpleasant characteristics. Such an attitude may easily sour human relationships, creating stress where none need exist. So, if we observe some attribute in another person which displeases us, causing us to dislike that person, we can use this as a sign suggesting we should observe ourselves to find if we, too, share this attribute.

Probably we will, for human beings are all pretty much alike. If we object to some behaviour of another person, the chances are very good that we have either done the same thing ourselves or, at least, wanted to do it. It is just that we do not put together the behaviour we dislike in the other person and our own behaviour. Once we can do so, it becomes easier to accept other people as they are. This makes for better human relationships and less distress in our lives.

Addictions and preferences

Upgrading addictions to preferences is another specific skill which enables us to reduce our stress level through playing the Inner Game more successfully. In the *Handbook to Higher Consciousness* Ken Keyes identifies addictions as unfulfilled desires caused by the external world not conforming to our demands. People like the world to be rational, reasonable and controllable by themselves. Unfortunately, the world is not like that. It was not created especially to give us whatever we demand, and therefore there will be many occasions upon which we will feel angry, frustrated and resentful because we are not getting what we want. That is, we experience considerable distress.

If I asked you, the reader, what are your addictions, you would probably answer 'alcohol' or 'cigarettes'. This is one way of looking at addictions. Another way, suggested in Keyes' book, is to define them in terms of anything which makes us upset, which rouses negative emotions in us. Also, anything about which we keep thinking, despite efforts to change our thoughts, can be seen as an addiction.

Evelyn Hayes has an addiction. A housewife, Evelyn wakes each morning to her clock radio broadcasting the news. As we well know, news services are usually litanies of disaster, detailing the latest miseries from all round the world. This recital of misery depresses her greatly, the reason being her belief that the world should be 'fair'. It is unfair that people should suffer, be exploited, die. True, it is, but Evelyn's addiction to a 'fair' world causes her to feel miserable and depressed. As long as she continues to be addicted in this way she will remain in this negative state for the world is not a 'fair' one and people will always be victimized in one way or another.

While Evelyn is addicted to a particular view of how the world should be, Barry Peterson expects his car always to work perfectly. One morning, Barry dashes into his garage only to find his front tyre flat. This situation provokes a storm of swearing and 'Why should this happen to me?'-type utterances. Such behaviour is the key indicator of an addiction. Whenever you feel angry, jealous, envious or frustrated, try to identify what is causing this emotional state. There you have your addiction, an obstacle which you have created in your mind that prevents you using your potentialities to the fullest extent and which generates great distress in your life.

Upgrading these addictions to preferences will enable you, together with Evelyn and Barry, to remove these obstacles. What does this involve? In Evelyn's case, instead of thinking, 'It is so unfair that people should die needlessly in a train smash in India. That makes me feel so sad and miserable', she would think, 'It is sad that people died needlessly in the train smash. I would prefer that it had not happened. However it has, and my worrying about it will alter nothing, achieve nothing except make me miserable.' Similarly Barry would put it this way, 'I would prefer it if my car tyre was okay and the car worked perfectly. However, the tyre isn't okay and I'll just have to change it. It won't help me to get upset and angry. That will make the job slower and damage my health.'

We are controlled to a great extent by the thoughts we accept, by the things we tell ourselves. If we insist on making demands on the world, and then become angry and upset when these demands are not met, we are in for a very frustrating life. Many people do live this way, labouring under the delusion that we have claims on life and that it is unjust if life does not grant these claims. Alternatively, we can *prefer* the world to be a certain way rather than demand it be so. Thus, we cannot lose. Either things go the way we want them to and we feel good, or they go badly and we refuse to become upset because it was only our preference, after all.

Acting in this way, we free ourselves, to a great

extent, from the control of people and other external conditions. If we are addicted to something happening in a particular way, we are under the control of outside forces which decide how that event will occur. Once we upgrade to a preference, we feel it would be nice if things turned out as we would like but we are not going to worry about it too much if they do not. We become less mechanical.

Evelyn and Barry have no choice at present. Once she hears of a disaster in the news, Evelyn is miserable. If Barry's car is not operative, he explodes in anger. Automatic reactions these—push button A and get response B. Addictions impose these; preferences do not. We have a choice of how we can react: if we want to get angry, we can. If we do not want to get angry, we realize a preference is something about which it is not worth becoming distressed.

Upgrading to preferences is really a matter of self-observation again. Look for the link between your distress and your demands and expectations. Probably when you are upset, angry or resentful you will find you are making requirements which the world cannot meet. Do you recognize: 'I will love you if you . . .' (and then follows a list of requirements necessary if the person is to provide his or her love)? Or, 'We will regain profitability when the economy improves' (or 'when the seasons become more reliable' or 'when people realize our produce is worth the extra money' or 'when the unions take a more responsible stance'). These requirements are rarely, if ever, met. They are plaintive pleas to the external world, asking it to change—and it is not going to do so just to please you. So forget the requirements and take life as your teacher. Let it show you your addictions so you can upgrade them to preferences and, by so doing, play the Inner Game with more chance of winning and of reducing your stress level.

Realistic expectations

Addictions, as described in the previous section, are really rigid expectations. We expect a certain result and, if we do not get it, we think it is awful, terrible, catastrophic. Albert Ellis in his *Guide to Rational Living* has pointed out that there are two unrealistic expectations which cause much of the distress in our lives. Brian Evans, a patient of mine, held both of these. Brian believed that he should do everything perfectly. If mistakes were made, he would agonize, inflating the incident out of all proportion to its seriousness. Obviously, Brian will be over-reacting a lot because people are not perfect and will be constantly making mistakes. That is, his expectation of perfection is quite irrational.

So, too, is his belief that he should be universally liked and that if people criticize him and are hostile, that is unfair and unjustified. No matter what we do and say, we will please some people and antagonize others. The trick is to maximize the former and minimize the latter. However, it is most unlikely that everyone will like us. Yet Brian expects that they should, and reacts negatively when this expectation is disappointed. His rigid belief system is thus creating internal obstacles which seriously interfere with his efficiency and increase the distress he experiences.

There is an alternative way to analyse situations which is likely to overcome obstacles created through an unrealistic belief system. Consider a specific example. Brian learns that his wife has made a mistake over a message he has asked her to deliver. He becomes very upset, and angrily castigates his wife for her error. Analysed according to Ellis' theory we would have:

A *The activating event* which is the mistake

B *Brian's belief system* that mistakes should never happen

C *The emotional consequence* of Brian's anger because a mistake has been made

> **D** *The dispute* whether B, the belief system, is rational or irrational.

Ordinarily we would assume that A causes C. Ellis' alternative proposal is that it is B, Brian's belief about A, which causes C. This is a very different situation, for the key issue now is D. Is this belief realistic or unrealistic? If the former is the case, then Brian's anger would seem justified. If the latter is true, then it would be inappropriate.

The important action for Brian to take, if he wants to reduce his too-high level of arousal, is to examine his belief system about the behaviour taking place at A. Self-observation is useful here, the adoption of a detached view. The inner 'I' sees the outer personality, Brian, making mistakes himself, therefore is it rational to expect others not to err? Some people will never, of course, adopt such a stance, never examine their belief system, either because they are so sure of their own correctness or because they fear it would not stand such examination.

Again, it is our emotional reaction which is the signal. Is this a realistic reaction to the event in question or is it unrealistic because our belief system is irrational? Are our expectations of ourselves and others reasonable, or does our belief system cause us to make these expectations quite unreasonable? Sometimes we may be demanding too much of ourselves, a sure route to increased distress. At other times we might be indulging ourselves because of a process called internal considering.

Internal considering

This term, coined by the Armenian 'guru' Gurdjieff, describes the situation where we feel we are unappreciated, our talents unrecognized. We are not properly treated or understood, and we tend in these circumstances to make accounts against other people

who are not valuing us appropriately. We feel
resentment and this introduces stress into any
relationship. We come to believe others owe us. This
idea is very like that of expecting the world to give us
what we want, of making requirements that are
necessary if we are to be happy. If you find yourself
using the word 'unfair' frequently, you can be
reasonably certain that you are internally considering.

Perhaps the most common form of internal
considering is where you believe everything is done to
you on purpose. George Ede has a very important
business luncheon. He hopes to secure an advertising
contract with a client whom he has been pursuing for
years. George wakes with a headache and, then, while
eating breakfast, spills milk over his freshly laundered
shirt. 'Why does it always have to happen to me?' he
wails. Sounds familiar? Then he is delayed by a phone
call and an unpunctual taxi so he arrives late at the
restaurant. Thrown off stride, George is far from
smooth in his presentation and the client leaves still
undecided about placing his account. True, George is
unlucky, but it is supreme vanity to believe that he has
been singled out by some mighty power for such
treatment.

Yes, many of us believe we are badly treated by fate,
that unfortunate events happen only to us while others
are treated so much better. By holding such a belief we
create considerable distress for ourselves, for we are
constantly justifying our failures in terms of 'bad luck'.
Unfortunately, the more we justify ourselves, the more
we are lying to ourselves, providing a convenient excuse
which prevents us observing ourselves more closely to
find out the real reasons for our failure to achieve the
success we desire.

We need to cancel these debts which we feel are owed
to us by life if we are ever to win the Inner Game.
Believing our failure is due to being treated improperly,
or not having met the right people, or having been let

down by others, only creates mental obstacles which place limits upon us, limits which do not have to be there when we realize how we can change. Most of us, for example, believe that our feelings for other people are relatively fixed. There are some people you like, others you dislike. That is the way it is. Or is it?

Changing your opinion of others

When we say we dislike someone, is our negative feeling directed towards the physical presence of that person? I believe not. What we are doing is reacting to the image in our minds which we have of that person. Often this image is a result of our first meeting, of the first few minutes we spent in his or her company. First impressions are very powerful, usually influencing us to distort or ignore later behaviour of the person which provides contradictory information. So this initial mental image is continually reinforced by later experience in which we tend to see what we want to see.

The image, though, only 'stands for' the disliked person, just as the thin blue line on the map represents a river. We have the power to change our image, and the feelings attached to it, by changing our map of the world. What we have been doing in the past is focusing upon the disliked person's bad points. Why not deliberately find his or her good points? They exist, you know. It is just that we have selectively tuned them out because our first impression has been unfavourable.

It is really not difficult to change focus in this way for, as I have pointed out earlier, the attributes we dislike in others are those we possess ourselves. Once we can accept this idea and ascertain its truth through self-observation, we are able to see the other person as being similar to ourselves. This makes it much easier to put ourselves in his or her position, realizing the difficulties involved—for they are difficulties we, ourselves, have faced. In fact, once you find the same thing in yourself that you have been finding in other people, your dislike is often cancelled out. This is extremely valuable for if, as Sartre says, 'Hell is other people', anything you can do to improve personal relationships is likely to make your life easier and less distressful.

The flexibility involved in changing your map of the world, of cancelling out dislikes and replacing them with neutrality or even liking, is a vital skill of the Inner Game. Without such flexibility we are locked into the same old patterns, at the mercy of the same old self-imposed obstacles and limitations. Change of attitude to another person is possible just as change of attitude towards your life in general is possible. This mental reprogramming provides the subject of the next chapter.

9 The Conscious Reprogramming of the Mind

Personal responsibility

Before we can reprogramme our minds, we need to accept that we are personally responsible for the greater part of our distress, that most of our problems are self-inflicted through the attitudes we choose to adopt and the ways we choose to think. It is true that flood, famine, war and other such traumatic events are outside our control and will exert a powerful influence over our state of mind. However, most of the time, no such external pressure is operating and, should we feel negative and depressed, this is primarily a function of our own approach to life. We have virtually no control over the external world, but we do have considerable power over the internal world of our minds. It is the use of this power to effect change which may be called mental reprogramming.

Such reprogramming may be conscious or subconscious. In the former case we deliberately change our thinking. We are quite aware of what we are doing. In the latter case, though we consciously prime the mind for change, we allow subconscious mental mechanisms to actually achieve this result. We are unaware of how the change is being carried out. That is, it takes place below the level of normal everyday consciousness. This second type of mental reprogramming will be considered in the next chapter.

In the present chapter we are concerned with conscious reprogramming. There is nothing particularly difficult about this as far as understanding the ideas involved. However, what is more difficult is putting them into practice. This is because knowledge alone is not enough to effect change. We already know how to live more successfully, to work better, to improve our human relationships. It is just that we do not put these things we know into practice. We read or hear certain ideas, think they sound pretty useful, but do nothing further about them. Perhaps we are lazy or apathetic. Maybe we are also too inflexible.

Earlier I commented on rigid belief systems. To illustrate how an inner obstacle of this sort can block change let us look at Bernard Scanlan. Bernard conducted a locum service for medical practitioners. He had completed several years of a medical course before deciding a business career interested him more than the practice of medicine. Having heard some radio publicity about my book, *The Healing Factor: A Guide to Positive Health*, Bernard came to a lecture I was giving on this subject. He remained afterwards to ask me about a particular problem. Though he functioned excellently in his office and on a one-to-one basis with his clients, he became very nervous when called upon to speak to a group of people. This did not happen very frequently but, whenever it did, Bernard virtually 'froze', finding it very difficult to speak coherently. He would stammer and sweat profusely, his pulse rate would increase, and generally, he would feel shaky and highly ill-at-ease.

Bernard asked me what he could do about his problem. I told him about a homoeopathic remedy, *Argentum Nitricum*, which has proved helpful in many cases where people become highly anxious in test-like situations. In mentioning homoeopathy, however, I could have saved my breath. 'Absolute rubbish' was Bernard's response. 'Homoeopathy doesn't work!' Now Bernard did not *know* that it would not work. He *believed* so because of things he had been told during his medical course. He had never tried a homoeopathic remedy, so he had no way of knowing whether it would help him. His rigid belief system, in other words, prevented him finding out.

Dismissal of ideas contrary to your existing beliefs is a sure way of ensuring you will never change, for it blocks you from exploring areas which may be of help to you. Therefore, I would suggest you try out for yourself the ideas to be now outlined before you decide whether they will or will not be helpful. Suspend disbelief, put aside your mental maps which tell you what is and is not possible, and simply experiment. If you give an idea a fair trial and it does not produce the results you want, then drop it and try something else. Results are what counts but do not reject a technique until you have tried it for yourself. Avoid rejecting it beforehand because your present belief system says, 'This cannot work'.

Placing your consciousness

Our minds are like cities. In a city there are the exclusive suburbs with beautiful houses and tree-lined streets. There are also slum areas where the houses are small and cramped and where greenery does not exist. We have slums in our minds, too. These are the dark areas of distress, miserable thoughts, of depression, of negativity. Conversely, there are the bright areas where we think positively, efficiently, happily. To a great extent, we can exert conscious control over where we place our thoughts.

Don Chamberlin is one who has learnt to do so. As manager of a supermarket, he has a myriad of day-to-day problems with which to contend. For several years he allowed those problems to dominate his life, for they occupied his thoughts, not only during the working day, but also at home. Because his anxious attention was so often fixed on problems, he was living mainly in the slum areas of his mind. Worried, anxious, depressed, Don was irritable with his family and unhappy with his life generally. He was a man under stress.

Then he fell ill. For six weeks he was away from work, away from the constant stream of troubles which normally flowed across his desk. After he got over his initial worry about what was happening at work, he started enjoying his enforced rest. His thoughts turned to pleasant things as he read escapist books and watched television. As his recovery progressed, he sat outside in his garden, enjoying the warmth of the sun, the pleasure of his children's company after school and the appreciation of returning strength.

When Don returned to work, the Transport Union was striking again. Goods were held up, supplies on the shelves were running short. Immediately, he slipped back into his old pattern. Irritability returned. One night his daughter pointed out how, within one week of his going back to work, he had become a different, far less pleasant person. This really shocked Don.

He consulted me, wanting some help on how he could improve the quality of his life. We talked of many things but the one which appealed most strongly was the idea of the conscious placement of attention. His present state was anxiety, worry and other negative feelings. What he wanted, his desired state, was calmness and positive feelings such as he had experienced when recovering from his illness. I asked him, 'What prevents you going from your present state to your desired state?' Don initially had no answer. Then he realized nothing was stopping him other than his lack of confidence in his ability to control his placement of consciousness.

After looking at his life experiences, Don understood he had always had this ability, yet had not realized it. Many times in his life he had consciously shifted his thoughts away from things which were upsetting him to others which were pleasure-inducing. However, these shifts had occurred randomly. He had made no attempt to apply the technique systematically.

So, Don practised a new habit. He learned to control his consciousness. Rather than place it in the slums of negativism, he directed it towards the exclusive suburbs of more positive, cheerful thinking. Not that his problems disappeared; of course they did not. However, because he no longer dwelled on them, seeing the worst and feeling overwhelmed, he found solutions more quickly. By deliberately allowing himself to focus on his problems for limited periods during the work-day, then switching his thoughts in more positive directions, particularly while at home, he gave his subconscious mind more opportunity come up with solutions. By the deliberate placing of consciousness, Don achieved a considerable degree of control over his attitudes and over his level of stress. Your attitude is in your own hands. It is yours for the making, even when the situation involves something as apparently un-changeable as time.

Time as a series of events

We tend to think of time as fixed and immutable. The past is past, the present is what we are now living, the future is yet to come. Yet we can expand or contract time in terms of the attitude we take.

Judith Seares works in an advertising office. Several years ago, Judith made a bad mistake. She lost her temper and insulted a client who withdrew his very large account from the firm. It was no use for Judith to realize the man was rude, indecent and actually deserved to be put in his place. Her action, though personally satisfying, had cost her firm a lot of money.

This incident was in the past. Thinking about it could achieve nothing, other than make Judith feel bad. Yet, dwell on it she did. In fact, it is still a major topic of her conversation, three years after it occurred. What Judith has done is take an incident which occupied a small slice of time and expanded it. She has made it occupy a considerable amount of her present life.

Conversely, James Harding has condensed time. A newspaper editor, he was badly injured in a car accident and became a paraplegic. For many months he was sunk in a sea of misery, depression and self-pity. Many similarly afflicted people remain in this state; James did not. He decided he would use what faculties he still retained to create something of value. Although he had not written fiction before his accident, James began 'writing' children's stories. He dictated these on to a dictaphone and his wife typed the manuscript from the tapes. Though not raging successes, the three books so far published have given him a reason for existence, a belief that he is bringing pleasure to many children. As a result, his whole attitude towards his incapacity has changed. He has, to a great extent, put it behind him and got on with living by refusing to talk and think about it. Just as Judith has expanded her mistake to fill a large part of her life, James has contracted his accident and physical condition so that they tend to drop out of his life. He tries to take his days one at a time in order to get as much out of them as he can.

Living in the present

By living one day at a time, concentrating on the present moment, James might well have discovered the secret of the productive life. Much of the self-destructive behaviour which produces so much stress in our lives is a result of attempting to live in a time other than the present. That is what Judith is doing. Her thoughts are continually in the past as she echoes and re-echoes the thought, 'If only I hadn't . . .'

This is a very destructive thought, as is its companion, 'What would happen if . . .?' This second question is the plaint of the person who is living in the future rather than the present. Although things might be going well at the moment, how long will this last? Something is sure to go wrong soon. So one person lives in the past, crying over spilt milk, and the other lives in the future, fearing impending disaster. All our regrets will not change the past, and the future cannot be lived until it arrives as the present moment. The nice thing about the future, too, is that it can only arrive one day at a time.

If it is the memories of the past and the fear of the future which makes our present so difficult, choose to live the 'now'. Each day may be considered as a life in itself. When we get up in the morning, we have been given the gift of a new day, a day which awaits us fresh and unspoilt. It is material waiting for us to shape in any way we want. If we insist on immediately picking up yesterday's burden of worry and anxiety, thinking of the day as a series of problems to be faced, that is our choice, but it is one we do not have to make. Here we have a fresh life, stretching from the time we wake until the time we fall asleep. We can, to a great extent, make it a rich, full life or one of unhappiness and worry.

It is amazing, too, what we can cope with for one day. Robert Louis Stevenson put it well when he said:

> Anyone can carry his burden, however hard, until nightfall.
> Anyone can do his work, however hard, for one day.
> Anyone can live sweetly, patiently, loving, purely till the sun goes down.
> And this is all life really means.

That is, we do not have to carry an ever accumulating burden of worry and anxiety forward from one day to the next. Each night spells the end of that life. We start fresh in the morning, unstressed.

This approach can change your whole attitude to existence. Jill Landers found this to be true. Jill found her sedentary life was doing terrible things to her waistline. She had tried eating less food but, always, she would have a bad day, perhaps overeating while feeling bored, throw up her hands and say, 'What's the use?' I encouraged Jill to take one day at a time. If she overate one day, she was given the opportunity to start fresh the next morning. Should she be able to reduce her food intake for one day, that meant she was able to lose weight. For what she could now do was begin anew the next day, and add this period of reduced eating to the one before. Seven such reductions equal a week. It is amazing how, by taking one day at a time, you can go week after week, month after month, gradually reducing your food intake without any real feeling of deprivation.

The same applies to becoming a non-smoker or reducing alcohol intake. The virtue of this approach is we feel we can handle almost anything for the short period between waking in the morning and falling asleep at night. Our problem is, too often, we think in terms of weeks, months, years and feel we could not possibly handle our problem, be it over-eating, running a business, smoking, or anything else, over that period of time. The burden would become too heavy.

What it really comes to is to concentrate on the challenge of the moment without allowing the past or future to interfere. This turns distress into eustress. Together with this attitude you might also like to accept whatever happens as what is. People, events, the weather, are what they are. If they displease you, that is too bad—but your displeasure is not going to change anything. It is more productive to accept that what is, is—but that you have the resources within you to change your attitude so you will not be unduly disturbed by outside events.

This is a return to a point made earlier, that external events and your reactions to those events are two different things. Whether you have developed a disturbed mind through regret over the past, or through fear and uncertainty about the future, or through dislike of a present situation, remember that it is usually the way you have choosen to react which is the problem, rather than the external events themselves. By consciously practising the ideas outlined in this chapter you can assume more control over your reactions. You can achieve this, too, through more subconscious processes.

10 The Subconscious Reprogramming of the Mind

Using trance states for self-development

All of us have the capacity to go into a trance. We do it every day of our lives when we day-dream or become so engrossed in a book, film or television show that we are unaware of our everyday surroundings. Basically, that is what trance is, a letting go of the actual physical environment and an entry into another world which exists in your mind. Perhaps this world in your mind is created by the book, film or television show, or perhaps you create it yourself through the use of your own imagination. It is this latter way of generating trance, and then the use of the state once it exists, that we shall be concerned with in this chapter.

Imagination really rules our lives. Unfortunately, as was pointed out earlier, we often use this marvellous gift to create distress for ourselves. In his capacity as a salesman, Len Bostock travels a great deal. Because of the distances involved, travel by air is a necessity—yet Len loathes flying. This is due mainly to the way he allows his imagination to work while he is in the plane: he always imagines the worst. Constantly attuned to the slightest change in the sound of the engines or to the effects of turbulence, Len 'sees' the plane crashing, causing his own death or injury. Consequently, the time he spends in the air is purgatory. Though he can be confronted with the safety record of airlines, the number of times he has flown without mishap, the far greater risk he runs in driving his car, Len remains locked into his fear. His imagination is more powerful than reality.

We saw this earlier when discussing fear of the future. We do not know what the future might bring, yet we constantly conjure up, in our imagination, 'pictures' of what might happen. These 'pictures' can then create as much fear and panic as if the real thing had actually occurred. Perhaps more so, for imagination can make cowards of us all.

How often do you think of all the things that could go wrong with a particular project you are planning? Once you start dwelling on the possible problems, your imagination can inflate them until they seem real to you. You forget that it is you who are creating these problems in your own mind, and come to accept that they really exist.

Thus, image comes to equal reality. We accept the creations of our imagination as really existing. This human capacity can, however, be very useful to us, working to our benefit just as effectively as it can work to our detriment. The key is to replace fear with desire. Instead of vividly creating mental pictures of what you fear, 'see' what you desire as if it were already yours.

This type of visualization can be described as success imagery. Though effective under many conditions, it seems to gain most power when done in such a way as to enlist the co-operation of the subconscious mind. Of course, we do not really know if we have 'two' minds. It just seems as if we do. Our conscious mind uses information supplied by our five senses to reason, think and plan. We are quite aware of it doing so. However, our subconscious mind seems to operate in ways not related to our physical senses, working more by intuition. It controls breathing, digestion and other involuntary operations of the body, appears to be a storehouse of memories of everything that has ever happened to us in our lives and is the home of the emotions.

It almost seems as if the subconscious mind functions somewhat like a computor in that it does not think for itself, but is capable of being programmed by our conscious mind. If we constantly feed in a diet of fearful, negative thoughts, our 'computor' will accept this data and cause us to act accordingly. Conversely, if we change the programme to a more positive one, our behaviour appears to change as a result.

The positive programming is very effectively achieved through use of the imagination while we are in a trance state. Apparently, the relaxed, dreamy quality of the trance, which is akin to the feeling we have just before we float off to sleep at night, enables us to contact our subconscious mind more readily. Thus, we can increase the power of our positive input. Let's see how Len could use this approach to change his fear of flying.

An example of reprogramming the mind

At the moment, Len is programming his mind on a diet of fear. Through his imagination, he is telling himself that he is likely to be killed or injured every time he flies. His subconscious mind has accepted this input and acts as if it were a true statement of the way Len's world is. Consequently, it ensures that he feels fear even at the mention of flying. To change this pattern, it is necessary to give Len's subconscious mind a new message, and to give it in such a way that it is powerful enough to override the earlier negative programme.

The initial step involves relaxation. One way to achieve this is for Len to sit comfortably in a chair and concentrate on his breathing rhythm. Without attempting to change this, he simply becomes aware of how his breath flows in and out. In itself, this is a relaxing process, for it tends to still the mind by giving it something to concentrate on. It can be made more effective if Len feels that as he exhales, each breath he lets go is carrying all tension, strain and worry out of his body. As this happens, he allows himself to let go, melting down in the chair.

We have already seen that 'allowing' is the key word here. We cannot make ourselves relax. It is something that happens quite naturally if we permit it. The concept of detachment mentioned earlier can be quite helpful. We 'stand-off', our inner 'I' watching the outer personality's breathing rhythm, relaxing it into a state of peaceful tranquillity.

Once his body is relaxing, Len allows himself to drift into a trance. Many people feel they do not know how to enter such a state but that is no problem. As Len sits in his chair, at the back of his mind, in his subconscious mind, there already exists the knowledge of how to enter trance. After all, he has done so thousands of times in his life already. If he really wants to change his feelings about flying, to let go of the fear, all Len has to do is go into a trance. This can be quite a deep state in which his mind seems to drift away from his body, to float easily in space accompanied only by the inner voice which will continue to give him directions. There is a feeling of safety and security as the mind floats, the body simply being left behind to continue relaxing with every breath exhaled. It is a lovely sensation.

To help the process along, Len may deliberately day-dream. One day-dream I have found particularly useful with many people is to create a sunken garden as a fantasy, using the steps leading down to it as a means of letting go of unwanted habits. Naturally, people will vary this according to their own interests but the following description might be a useful starting point.

Len is to imagine himself on the patio of a beautiful

house. There are ten steps leading down to the sunken garden. As he goes down each step he lets go a little more, becoming increasingly calm and relaxed. Also, with each step he lets go of the fear, allowing it to melt away into nothingness. When he reaches the garden, Len is feeling a marvellous sense of tranquillity and stillness.

The garden may be full of brightly coloured flowers, a few trees, freshly cut lawn and perhaps a fountain. As well as 'seeing' these things, or anything else he would prefer in his garden, Len may 'hear' the splash of falling water from the fountain, the singing of birds in the trees and the buzzing of bees around the flowers. Possibly he might be able to 'smell' the flowers or the freshly cut lawns, and to 'feel' the warmth of the sun soaking into his body. By making his garden as vivid as possible, Len creates the state of internal absorption which is so much a feature of the trance state.

Once this state of calm and stillness is present, Len uses his imagination further to provide his success imagery. He 'sees' himself taking a plane trip—the way he would like it to be. Calm, confident and comfortable, he is enjoying relaxing back into his seat, sipping a cool drink, and observing the people around him. Time is passing very quickly and it is with a sensation of surprise that he finds the plane descending. The trip has been so fast. By imagining the successful flight or flights while in a trance state, Len is programming his mind to accept that this is the sort of person he is, one who travels by air comfortably and enjoyably.

The more vivid the imagery, the more powerful the programming. This means using pictures, sounds, feelings and smells, or as many of these as possible. However, even if your imagining is limited to one sense only, your chances of success are high for, when the mind is calm and the body relaxed, the subconscious mind is very impressionable. As I've pointed out, it does not seem to distinguish between imagination and reality. Therefore, the images Len puts into his mind, images of successfully coping with flying, are accepted as real. If Len continues this imagery as he falls asleep each night and during other periods of deliberate relaxation, by the time he comes to fly again his mind will have already accepted that he has flown successfully many times before and this is just one more time.

Repetition is important. Although I know of some people who have achieved successful reprogramming after only one or two 'sessions', most of us require longer to change the negative effects of previous input. I would suggest you begin with a session like that outlined for Len, then repeat the success imagery every night as you fall asleep for two weeks. In addition, repeat the relaxation session several times over those two weeks.

Incidentally, it is very important to always have positive, optimistic, cheerful thoughts in your mind as you fall asleep at night for you are actually drifting into a trance state at this time. This means your subconscious mind is very susceptible. If you worry over the day's problems, stirring up anxiety and other negative feelings, you are programming yourself in a very self-defeating way. Conversely, an input of positive imagery before sleep should ensure pleasant dreams, uninterrupted rest and realization in actuality of the things you are picturing.

I have stressed images rather than words, for the subconscious mind appears to respond more readily to them. However, if you are unable to create mental pictures, and many of us are unable to do so, tell yourself the things you want to hear, think the thoughts of the success you desire. In fact, it is desirable to combine both the visual and the verbal to achieve maximum effectiveness. If you do so during the trance periods, you are likely to achieve a great deal, certainly more than you would have by doing the same thing during non-trance periods.

Acting as-if

To enhance the effect of your subconscious mental programming, there is further action you can take on a conscious level. Shakespeare put it well when he said: 'Assume a virtue, if you have it not.' This is a poetic way of advising you to act *as-if* you are already the person you want to be.

Dan Fowler found this worked really well. His problem was that he lacked confidence in himself. Unfortunately, he showed it. He could be easily overawed by both associates and competitors, often failing to volunteer ideas to his superiors, stumbling over his words during meetings, and really feeling he had been very lucky to have achieved his position as manager of the country branch of a firm selling motor parts.

After I discussed subconscious mental programming with Dan, and guided him through a session similar to that described for Len, he was able to imagine himself in a number of situations acting with confidence and self-assurance. He 'saw' himself as he would like to be, handling other people courteously but firmly, offering ideas to his superiors in the city headquarters of the firm, speaking quietly and confidently at meetings.

He practised this imagery for several weeks. As he did so, he made a conscious effort to be the person he was imagining himself to be. To get over his awe of colleagues and competitors he believed to be better than himself, Dan continually reminded himself that they put on their pants one leg after the other just as he did. Perhaps he would even image them in ludicrous situations such as sitting up in the bath with a feather sticking out of their nose. Imagination again, but used constructively to help Dan act as if he was the equal of anyone with whom he came in contact.

The same ploy of imagining people in ways which reduce their awe-inspiring aura helped him handle himself better at meetings and in marshalling the confidence to offer suggestions to his superiors in the firm. He began playing a part, the part of a poised, confident businessman, one who was aware of his own abilities and comfortable in any situation. As any actor knows, when he plays a role, he very quickly assumes the characteristics of the person he is portraying. Often, his difficulty is divorcing himself from the role once the performance is over.

This is what Dan found, though he had no desire to leave the role after playing it at a meeting or interview. In other words, by starting out pretending to be the person he wanted to be, he became that person. It was pretence no longer. With Dan, the process took only three or four weeks and he found that, as his confidence grew, his earlier distress was transformed into eustress. His work became a stimulating challenge.

The secret is to have a vivid picture in your mind of what you want. This is the essence of your success imagery, to create a clear goal or target at which to aim. Once you know what you want, programme your subconscious mind to achieve it, and then act as-if you have already achieved it by doing whatever is necessary to transform yourself. By acting as-if you are a success, you become a success.

Nowhere is this more clearly demonstrated than in sales interviews. Research has suggested that the first four minutes of contact between salesmen and prospective customers is vital. Therefore, the salesman might well use his subconscious programming to 'see' himself handling the early part of the interview particularly effectively. He would be dressed appropriately, smile frequently, maintain steady eye contact and greet his prospective customer with a firm handshake. In addition, he would exude an air of optimism rather than one of pessimism. This would be his feeling internally, too, for we do seem to get what we expect, optimism anticipating success and pessimism anticipating failure.

Having created the clear mental image of his behaviour during the interview, but particularly the first four minutes, our salesman proceeds to act that role. If he has difficulty maintaining eye contact, and many of us do, he focuses his attention on the bridge of the other person's nose. Even though he is looking at a spot between the person's eyes, it seems as if he has a steady eye-to-eye gaze which can be most impressive. By playing the role, he immerses himself in it and not only enhances his chance of a sale but also contributes to a permanent personality change.

Changing life history

This can be achieved in other ways, too, such as changing personal history. Rosalyn Hughes wanted to change her touchiness, her aggressive reaction to quite innocent comments which she interpreted as being critical of her. Fortunately it is possible to change a distress-creating response like this with a very simple technique. Again, it involves both conscious and subconscious elements. Usually, a therapist guides a patient through the procedure but it can be accomplished alone.

The technique involves a person in finding some personal resource, such as confidence, relaxation, assertiveness, which he or she did not have at a particular time when he or she coped badly with some situation. This is then 'taken back' to change the situation and the negative feelings associated with it. In Rosalyn's case, she knows the maladaptive response she wants to change, this being her aggressive reaction to innocent comments which she construes as critical.

Relaxing in a chair, Rosalyn closes her eyes and 'enters into' the situation in which she has made this response. In her mind, she relives a specific time when she has behaved that way, attempting to actually experience the unpleasant feelings which are part of the situation. As she does so, she 'anchors' these feelings.

When a person is working alone with this technique as Rosalyn is she can, say, use the thumb of her right hand to touch her left wrist. This will serve as an anchor so that on any further occasion, when Rosalyn touches her wrist in this way, it will evoke the unpleasant feelings of her inappropriate aggressive behaviour.

Rosalyn then explores her experience to discover a positive resource which she possesses, one capable of changing the original, unpleasant situation to produce a more pleasing result. Perhaps, she has developed an ability to take herself less seriously, to laugh at herself, which she did not have when her aggressive behaviour first began. Or, maybe, she can find an episode in her life, preferably over the last two or three years, in which she handled a difficult situation as a mature, confident woman, achieving a feeling of success and satisfaction.

Should Rosalyn have been unable to think of any resource to 'take back', or any recent success experience, an alternative is available. This is to imagine how an admired person would handle the situation and to 'see' oneself acting in this way. This admired person may be someone actually known or even an historical character.

Rosalyn's resource was self-acceptance. She realized she was able to accept her competency without having to be constantly alert to possible attacks upon it. She felt she now had a self-assurance which made her present sensitivity unnecessary. She enjoyed imagining herself in situations which she had handled with poise and maturity. As she experienced the good feelings associated with these thoughts, she 'anchored' them by touching her left thumb with the little finger of her right hand.

Finally, Rosalyn brought her two sets of feelings together. Firstly, she touched her wrist to re-evoke the unpleasant feelings of the unwanted situation. Once these were present, she triggered her second 'anchor', the thumb, to bring in the resource and the pleasant feelings associated with it. She then sat quietly, eyes closed, until she experienced herself responding in a new way to the previously unpleasant situation. This new response she then generalized to any future situation similar to the one in which she had previously responded badly, by saying to herself, 'Any time I encounter anything similar to my previously unpleasant experience I will feel "this" ' (touching her resource 'anchor').

It is difficult to explain why this technique, which is far easier to do than to describe in words, works so well. In some way, the bringing together of the two sets of feelings, negative and positive, engages subconscious processes which work towards change in the desired direction. Many people have found, often to their amazement, that previously disruptive behaviour and the unpleasant feelings associated with it have virtually disappeared as a result of using this simple procedure. They have, in short, found a way of banishing an important source of distress.

Remaking the day

Fortunately, there are other procedures, even more simple, which will enable you to handle your life more successfully. Many of these I have described in *The Plus Factor: A Guide to Positive Living* and there is one I would like to repeat here as I feel it is particularly suited to reducing stress levels.

It involves an imaginative remaking of your day so it becomes 'perfect'. Earlier in this chapter I described the use of success imagery while in a trance state and also mentioned the importance of your choice of thoughts as you fall asleep at night. Remaking the day makes use of both these ideas.

In bed at night, as you prepare for sleep, let your mind drift back over the day's events. Think fully of the things you have done well. Run each one over in your mind several times, congratulating yourself on the way you have handled these situations. Next, consider those things which have not gone well. Select one, wipe it out of your mind, and replay the incident several times the way you would have preferred it to have gone. Make it right, in other words. Then, move on to the next situation and repeat the process, 'seeing' yourself, as vividly as possible, handling it successfully.

Probably you will fall asleep while making your day perfect in this way. That is all right, for what you are doing is programming your mind very positively so that the subconscious continues to work on this material while your conscious mind is asleep. However, if you find you fall asleep so quickly that you are unable to do the exercise, then perhaps when you awaken in the morning, still drowsy, would be a better time. Failing this, you can set aside a period each day during which you relax and remake the previous day at that time.

Incidentally, the fact that you are inclined to fall asleep easily while doing this exercise at night suggests that it is an excellent remedy for insomnia. Should you be a person who falls asleep easily, but then wakes during the night, you can now welcome those wakeful periods. Use them to remake your day and, not only will you find that your ability to handle your work improves, but you will also find you fall asleep again very quickly.

By using this procedure you will condition your mind in such a way that, increasingly, you actually behave in the way you desire. The inefficient behaviours drop out, because you are wiping them out of your mind the way you would wipe them off a blackboard, and the efficient behaviours become part of you because you are mentally rehearsing them so often.

Letting go of the 'rubbish'

Using this technique is one way of removing unwanted behaviours and feelings. Several others are worth your consideration also. One of these has you mentally going into your sanctuary, a quiet place such as the garden described earlier, and standing there with a wicker basket at your feet. The basket is open and into it you can dump everything you want to get rid of. This might include the inner obstacles of fear, doubt, anxiety, and guilt mentioned earlier, people who frustrate you, excess weight, cigarettes and anything else you feel diminishes your life and inhibits the expression of your true potentiality.

Once you have 'got rid' of everything you want to into the basket, imagine yourself shutting the lid and fastening it. You walk a couple of paces away and find a huge balloon attached by a cord to a metal peg in the ground. Untie it from the peg, carry it across to your basket and tie it to the handle in the lid. Then let it go. As the balloon floats into the air, taking away the basket and all the things you want removed from your life, you will feel a marvellous sense of release, a joyous feeling of letting go. This feeling grows stronger and stronger as the balloon floats higher until it, the basket, and its contents disappear out of your mind and out of your life.

For really troublesome things, some repetition of this procedure may be necessary. Alternatively, you might like to burn, bury, or otherwise destroy unwanted material. It does not really matter how you do it as long as it works. Always it is results that count, and that is particularly true of the way you manage other people.

11 Managing Other People

Manipulation—and behaviour modification

We do not like the word 'manipulation'. It has connotations of forcing people to do things we want but they do not want. Yet, in almost everything we do, we cannot avoid manipulating or being manipulated. At work, if you want others to discharge certain duties, you find ways of having them do so. In your home life, you try to have your spouse and children behaving in the way you want them to. If they do not, you seek methods of influencing them so that they do. That is manipulation. Whether we call it something different or refuse to acknowledge what we are doing does not alter the fact that, throughout our life, we try to manage other people so our needs are more adequately met and our stress level reduced.

In an earlier chapter I mentioned the value of making other people feel important, perhaps through helping them meet their needs and telling them things about themselves which they like to hear. These are ways of having others do as you desire them to do. You are attempting to assume control over their behaviour. We can decry this as inhuman, as undesirable, but in the very act of maintaining this we will find we are busy coercing our children, or bullying our secretary. It is the point about contradictions in our behaviour rising again. On the one hand we talk about every person's right to freedom, to make his or her own decisions, while on the other hand we try to make sure he or she exercises this freedom and makes these decisions in the way we want.

There is nothing wrong with this. It is just the way things are. However, if we do not recognize that this is the way the world works we place ourselves at a considerable disadvantage. By bending over backwards to avoid any suggestion that we are coercing others, we become prime targets for manipulation ourselves, and being manipulated is a very stressful experience. One side of the coin is to realize you can systematically use certain techniques to get others to do your bidding, and for them to actually enjoy doing so. The other side of the coin is to accept that others are trying to manipulate you into doing what they want, and to realize you can protect yourself against this if that is what you wish. For you may welcome this manipulation because it is helping you achieve something beneficial. Manipulation is neither good nor bad in itself. It is the end to which it is directed which can be seen in such value terms.

Behaviour modification is one such neutral technique which can produce both good and bad results. Possibly the most effective way of influencing other people is to reward them when they do as you want and ignore them when they do not do so. James Barry does not understand this basic principle of human functioning. A rather bad-tempered man, James often 'blasts' his secretary for making typing and shorthand errors. She does not do this often, but each time it occurs James becomes very angry, often reducing her to tears. When he cools down after his outburst, he feels contrite and usually buys her a little present to salve his guilty feelings.

What behaviour is James strengthening with this action? The behaviour of making mistakes and crying. After all, it is through making errors and crying that the secretary is rewarded with a gift. This strengthening of the wrong response is very apparent in the way parents

often interact with their children. Two little boys meet
in the street:

'Hi, Graeme, where did you get the chocolate?'

'Mummy bought it for me because I cried.'

'You mean your mummy *wants* you to cry?'

'I suppose so. Every time I cry she gives me
chocolates or biscuits or icecreams.'

'Gee, I'd cry a lot more if my mummy would give me
chocolates and icecream when I did.'

Ridiculous, isn't it? Surely, no intelligent, reasonable
parent would act this way. But they do, repeatedly. So
do smart, capable executives as they actually encourage
their employees to do the very things they do not want.
James, instead of strengthening his secretary's mistake-
making and crying behaviour, could completely ignore
her when she behaved in this way, acting as if she did
not exist. This is likely to be more effective in reducing
and eliminating the unwanted behaviour than punishing
her with an angry outburst. Strangely enough, human
beings seem to be less damaged by punishment than by
being ignored. When someone punishes us, at least he or
she demonstrates that he or she recognizes our existence
as a person. However, by ignoring us, he or she refuses
to acknowledge this existence. We are just not there, not
worthy of being recognized.

James' wife could turn this principle to good use if
she wished to modify his bad temper and have a more
peaceful home life. Every time he ranted and raved,
exploding over trifles as was his wont, she could simply
ignore him, continuing doing whatever she was doing
without acknowledging his existence. Not an easy thing
to do, perhaps, but possible—and well worth the effort
for the result produced. Conversely, whenever James
was pleasant and good-tempered, she could be
attentive, rewarding, pleasing him by doing those things
she knew he liked.

Similarly, in his office, the time for James to give his
secretary recognition, gifts, praise, would be on those

occasions when she had completed some really good work. It is so simple, really, yet we consistently increase the behaviour we do not want by ignoring the power of the principle that we continue doing those things for which we are rewarded while ceasing to do those things for which we are ignored.

The use of praise and flattery

Speaking of rewards, praise and flattery are among the most powerful of these. We all need strokes, those kind words and actions which help us to feel happier about ourselves. Even the most self-reliant, independent person feels warmed by the comment that he or she is doing something well. As a therapist and consultant, I am being continually 'stroked' by the success of people I have shown how to make more of themselves. Their positive changes, the joy they find in these, is tremendously rewarding. We all like to feel we matter, that what we do is of value. Praise and flattery, even if insincere, affirm that our efforts are recognized.

Because most people are so insecure, such strokes may produce effects out of all proportion to their intent. That is why even insincere flattery can produce beneficial effects. Of course, we would like to think that we, ourselves, flatter others only when we mean it, and that others do the same to us. This is preferable, but sometimes forcing oneself to be a little insincere, just for the sake of making someone else feel better, seems a small price to pay. However, most of the time, such insincerity is unnecessary, for it is not difficult to find things to praise about people.

Jim Trembath, a hospital attendant, practised this positive 'stroking' of people quite systematically. Every day, he made it a rule to say or do something nice for someone else on at least five occasions. Sounds almost schoolboyish, yet the effects were magical. Because Jim came in contact with many people during the day, and tried to help each one of these people feel better in some way or another as a result of their meeting, he created a ripple effect. If he complimented a woman employee on her dress, that woman experienced a lift in mood which, in turn, predisposed her to say something pleasant to the next few people she met. They in turn passed on the good feelings.

Many readers may feel this idea is too simple to work—and would not even try it. Sad, really. So many of us reject ideas without testing them. This deliberate giving of praise, of finding opportunities to flatter people, is an incredibly powerful technique for improving morale within any institution. I have used it successfully myself, or caused it to be used, in hospitals, schools, business firms and public service departments. It never fails. Even one person determined to say and do positive things for as many other people as possible can start the revolution. However, if a group decides to behave in this way, their power is irresistible.

Often the flattery and praise used need not be direct. You do not have to say always, 'Gary, you're doing a really good job on that design. I appreciate the extra care you are taking.' Instead, use a third person. Praise Gary's work to someone else who you are pretty sure will pass on the information. In fact, praise received from a third person in this way is often accepted by the recipient as more meaningful than direct praise.

Even remembering a person's name is valuable, for, to him, that is the most important sound in the language. You can also help the person feel important by giving him a good reputation to live up to. Knowing his work, it is not difficult to comment favourably upon it, and make him feel he is highly regarded by colleagues and competitors. This is easy, of course, with a capable man or woman. It is far less so with someone whose work is inadequate. The ploy really is inappropriate under such circumstances.

Yet, it is a peculiar quirk of human beings how they strive to live up to a reputation. When David Harris assumed control of an electronic firm, morale was quite low, particularly among the workers making stereo components. David talked to this group, pointing out that they were starting afresh. He was not interested in previous troubles or work records, all that counted was the present. Having read their personnel records he felt confident they were competent people with real skill who had the ability to help him improve the company's reputation. By giving them something to live up to and by expressing his faith in the workers, David helped them to feel an increased sense of pride in themselves, one which was reflected in improved production.

Acting as David did is the reverse of giving a dog a bad name. We tend to get what we expect from people. Expect the best—you will often get it, and this is certainly preferable to expecting the worst. Others pick up from us, usually non-verbally, what our expectations are and they react to these almost unconsciously. So, perhaps, it is good policy to give others a good reputation. They just may live up to it.

Asking for advice, opinions, and favours is another way of feeding a person's need for importance. By doing so, you indirectly suggest that he or she is powerful and influential, in a position to help you if he or she so desires. Interestingly enough, when you request a favour of someone influential, he or she will then often take an interest in your career. After all, you have indicated you recognize his or her importance, and this engenders friendly feelings which could work very much to your advantage.

So, too, does imputing knowledge and experience to others. While talking about a recent trip abroad, you could say something along the lines of, 'I know you've been to Italy too, George, and I'd appreciate your comment on this', or 'You've had a lot of experience in travelling overseas, Joan, would you share some ideas with us?' Just a variation on the theme of making others feel important but, the more ways you learn to do so, the better your human relationships become and the less stress you feel in being with other people.

The other side of the coin—criticism

Using praise and flattery to give positive 'strokes', recognition and a sense of importance is rather straightforward, but how can you give criticism in such a way that you maintain good relations with other people? Personally, I have found the 'sandwich' method to work well. When it is necessary to offer criticism, first endeavour to find something to praise. Begin in this way, by giving 'strokes', then introduce the criticism. Explain this clearly and quietly before concluding with something else positive. You accomplish two things by working in this way.

Firstly, you allow the other person to save face. You have not made it necessary for him to defend himself or to attack you. Rather, the way you have put it indicates your appreciation of his good work coupled with a suggestion as to how he can make it even better.

Secondly, your criticism is likely to produce better performance. When you focus your suggestions for improvement on just one or two points, you provide the other person with a manageable task. He is likely to feel, 'If I just improve in these couple of ways I can be doing a really fantastic job.' This approach is in marked contrast to that of many teachers, for example, who return student essays with a mass of criticisms and no praise. Students virtually give up, feeling there is just too much they need to improve. They have no hope. So, whenever you are tempted to unload a flood of criticism on someone, realize that probably all you'll achieve is to make yourself feel better. You are unlikely to help the other person improve.

The saving of face mentioned above is important. If you give the other person no opportunity to salvage his pride, you virtually ensure you have made an enemy who will then obstruct you in any way he or she can.

Provide an 'out'. Indirect criticism is a way of doing so, particularly by means of stories.

What you do is construct a tale which parallels the other person's present situation. The problem and its difficulties have a place in the story. So, too, do the people involved. However, the problem might be similar, but not identical; the people's relationships comparable, but their names different. In the story, criticism of a person's actions may be made, improvement suggested, and a problem solution based on these formulated.

The beauty of such an approach is that the person being criticized has no need to defend or justify himself. It is just a story, with things happening to someone else. In fact, he may not even recognize it as a criticism if the story is sufficiently subtle. However, what he is likely to do is engage in a process termed 'transderivational search', in which he explores his own experience and relates the events of the story to this. He makes personal meaning of the tale, sometimes at a subconscious level, and this enables him to effect the improvements required. This is quite a fascinating approach for the user and one which often produces most gratifying results.

So does the very simple behaviour of admitting your own mistakes—that you can be wrong too. Actually the things other people do about which we become upset are things we have usually done ourselves. It is just that either we have not remembered doing them or, through the blocking mechanism discussed earlier, have not recognized this particular facet of our own behaviour. So if you can relate a story in which you made the same mistake as the person you need to rebuke, you are likely to make your point effectively and do so without arousing too much resentment.

In the same vein, it is necessary to respect the opinions of others. We all have different models of how the world works, different maps of the territory in our heads, and ours may be lacking in some areas. What we see as an error deserving of harsh criticism may not be so. At least we should wait until we have talked with the other person, attempted to get some idea of how he or she sees things, before turning on the critical blast.

Having said all this, I do know there will be times when the pleasant, face-saving approach does not work. Then, it is necessary to be tough, hard, brutal. I've always believed that it is the outcomes we produce that provide our measure of success. I'd prefer to use resentment-minimizing techniques first. They make life easier all round. They reduce tension. Should they produce the desired results, well and good. If they do not, then try something different. That is the mark of the really successful person. When something does not work, they try something else, and keep doing so until they get the outcome they are after.

Assertive skills

Producing the outcomes you want is largely a matter of managing other people effectively. It is important for you to find ways of positive 'stroking', criticizing, and generally manipulating behaviour to achieve results minimizing distress. So, too, is being able to assert yourself, for being imposed upon is very distressful for most people. This can be difficult, probably more so for women than for men. From infancy, women are trained to be submissive, docile, unassuming, virtually taking what men are kind enough to give them. However, many men do not find it easy to assert their rights, beliefs or ideas either.

Assertiveness is not aggressiveness. It is simply the quiet insistence on being treated as a valuable and responsible person. To become a person able to assert yourself involves the practice of certain skills. These have been well explained by Manuel Smith in *When I Say No, I Feel Guilty*. They are four in number.

Broken Record is the first of these. All it means is that

you calmly repeat what you want, over and over again if necessary. Side issues are ignored, no reasons or excuses are given. You just state your point clearly and often.

Early in my academic career I was involved in educational staff meetings. One participant was a scholarly philosopher with a fearsome reputation for logical argument. I would sit in awe, hardly daring to open my mouth, as I saw him demolish other people's arguments.

However, it gradually dawned on me how he was doing this. He would take another person's argument, change it subtly and then destroy this changed version. Because of his incredible ability with words, the victim was unable to affirm he had actually said something different.

Rather hesitantly at first, I began using what I now recognize as the Broken Record technique. I would advance an idea briefly, and I hope, clearly. The philosopher, Noel, would enter into a long discourse about it, finally indicating its untenability. I would come back with, 'I can understand how you feel that way Noel, but that is not really what I said. What I said was . . .' This would trigger off another verbal flow. When it abated, I'd say, 'Yes, I see what you mean. However, it is not an answer to what I said. What I did say was . . .', and so on. Gradually, Noel's verbal flow would abate, he would turn purple, and finally subside. It worked like a charm as long as I noted down exactly the point I wanted to make and kept repeating it.

It is worth remembering this approach next time people try to sidetrack you or distract you from your purpose. Quietly and gently accept their right to their opinions, then restate your own point. Perhaps you may acknowledge what they are saying as useful, but remain your own judge of what to do. This is a second skill called *fogging*. Perhaps you have decided to approach a certain builder to do some alterations on your home. You have seen the work of a number of builders, studied all the information you can secure, and made a judgment based on this. The decision is yours and you will have to bear the responsibility if it turns out badly.

A friend, without the same access to the information you have, tells you stories he has heard about the firm you have chosen. Your response is, 'You may be right, but I still feel . . .' Additional information surfaces, but not strongly enough to outweigh that which you already possess, 'Yes, that seems right, but I still feel . . .'

I'm not suggesting you ignore all advice. Listen carefully, but make your own decision rather than letting others make it for you. Remember, it is you who has to live with it. The world is full of experts telling you how to run your life and your business. If they are wrong, and they very frequently are, it is you who suffer the consequences, not they. It's 'Well, back to the drawing board' for them.

A third assertive skill relates to a point made earlier—accept your errors and faults by agreeing with them. This is *negative assertion*. It is probable that most criticism has some element of truth so it is reasonable to simply accept this quietly and calmly. It saves arguments, too.

You can take this approach further with a fourth skill, *negative inquiry*, by which you actively prompt criticism in order to find out the real reason your behaviour upsets your critic. 'You're selfish,' says your wife, as you head for the closet to get your golf clubs. 'Why am I selfish?' you ask. 'I've been working all week and I'd like to have some relaxation.' Your wife keeps saying this is selfish, criticizing you for your behaviour. You keep probing until you get at the real reason for the criticism. She wants you to take her shopping. Once you arrive at the real reason, and it might take a long time, you have to choose whether to assert your right to use your time as you wish, or to agree she does see very little of you and this is a good opportunity to be together. By bringing the real reason for dispute out in the open, you can usually defuse it and minimize the distress which would occur if it dragged on day after day.

A point about selfishness: if you are accused of selfishness, all this really means is you are doing something someone else does not want you to do. The accusation of selfishness is designed to make you feel guilty, so that you will then accede to the other person's wishes. This other person would, of course, strongly deny that he or she was selfish for wanting to make you do what he or she wanted. As I have said, other people have faults. We have virtues.

Guilt is a marvellous means of manipulation. It is possibly the most effective means of all, rivalled only by anxiety and ignorance. If you want someone to do your bidding, make them feel guilty about not doing so. 'I know you were looking forward to having a game of golf, but the children see so little of you nowadays', or 'I'm desolate you feel so negatively about this idea for our new advertising campaign. I've spent so long in developing it, stayed up nights, given up my weekend', are typical examples. I am sure you recognize the pattern.

Alternatively, you might care to rouse fear and anxiety within someone's breast. 'You know, Charlie Bloggs followed the same diet you are starting.' 'Whatever happened to Charlie? Is that right? He really became quite ill. Amazing!' Such ploys are usually real winners in manipulating others to drop ideas you disapprove of and agree with solutions you provide.

Or you may prefer to make your 'opponent' feel stupid. Shop assistants frequently practise this one. As you take back the electrical appliance which does not work you are asked, 'Have you plugged it into the socket?' or 'Did you turn on the switch?' In other words, you are an idiot who probably did something stupid. That is why the appliance does not work, rather than anything being wrong with it. People can be intimidated into not complaining about faulty goods by such tactics. They are, then, usually quite distressed about their lack of courage in asserting themselves.

Perhaps you do not want to manipulate people through guilt, fear and ignorance. Still, remember others will be doing it to you, consciously or unconsciously, so learn to recognize the signs so you can defend yourself. Probably, the best defence is to bring it out into the open. 'Look, I know you are trying to make me feel guilty about playing golf. Still, I feel I'm entitled to some relaxation today. How about going out to dinner tonight?'

Manipulating people so that both they and you benefit is a most effective way of transforming distress into eustress. When everyone gains you feel good about what you have done, and as a result feel more at ease with yourself. That is what this book is about, turning dis-ease and distress into ease and eustress. The final chapter summarizes the main ways in which this might be achieved.

12 Conclusion

The counterstress philosophy

In *Stress Control*, Coleman summarizes the way in which stress may be successfully managed. Knowing your enemy is of vital importance: this means you, personally, must identify the factors causing your distress. Unless you know what is raising your blood pressure, creating your ulcer, or keeping you awake at night, you cannot take action to protect yourself. However, once you have identified the factors which cause distress in your life, you can estimate whether the advantages involved outweigh the disadvantages. Understand and accept those factors which offer worthwhile benefits or are unavoidable, but, as far as is possible, remove those which are harmful to you.

Knowing your enemy is important. So, too, is knowing yourself. Coleman stresses that to understand how the pressures and demands of your environment affect your life, you must understand your own perceptions, motives, ambitions and habits. Remember, you make your world by the way you think and the choices you make.

By deriving satisfaction from the four areas of home, work, hobby and friends, you greatly increase your ability to withstand pressures from the outside world. To survive successfully, Coleman suggests you fight only the important battles and ignore the trivial ones. Things are worth what you make them worth, and by wasting your energies in arguments over trifles you create distress for yourself. Be selective in how you expend your energy. Should your work be demanding, ignore attempts to persuade you to give your time to local politics or charitable organizations. Such extra activity may be sufficient to take your arousal level into the distress area. However, should your work be undemanding, seeking challenge in other activities may be very valuable.

This is all part of planning a defence strategy against over-stressing yourself. Learn how to relax by following the ideas outlined in earlier chapters, ensure that you allocate time for rest and hobbies, and maintain a good level of physical fitness. Exercise frequently, avoid over-indulgence in tobacco, alcohol and other drugs, and eat properly.

Eating properly is really a matter of a balanced diet including plenty of fibre, fresh fruits, fresh vegetables, and nuts, as well as fish and meat. Foods such as wheat-germ, lecithin, liver, yeast, kidneys and soy flour are particularly valuable in contributing to the health of the body and strengthening it so it is more capable of withstanding distress. All foods rich in the Vitamin B group, especially B5 and B6, Vitamin C and Vitamin E, are claimed to be helpful as stress preventers. So, too, are foods rich in the minerals calcium, potassium, zinc, magnesium and phosphorus. Herbs such as scullcap, passionflower, valerian and ginseng have been used for centuries to serve the same purpose.

Evidence is accumulating that food and mood would appear to be linked. A recent United Kingdom study, for example, has indicated that tryptophan, an amino acid present in meat, eggs and milk, may be just as successful in the treatment of depression as leading anti-depressant drugs. Such work is in its infancy, but it has been established for many years that homoeopathic remedies made from natural substances are effective in helping people handle pressure more effectively. In *The Healing Factor* I have talked of these remedies in some detail, particularly Kali Phos, Gelsemium and Argentum Nitricum which are proven 'tranquillizers'. Their great virtue is that they exert their calming influence without the negative side-effects found so frequently in modern tranquillizing drugs. The Bach flower remedies, Impatiens and Vervain, also fulfill this function of helping people relax without unwanted side-effects.

Selye's prescription

Any book on stress must draw heavily on the work of Hans Selye, the man who, virtually single-handed, made this topic 'respectable' as an area of research. I have used many of his ideas in previous chapters, and I feel it is fitting to conclude this book with his prescription for enjoying a full life.

- Admit there is no perfection, but in each category of achievement something is tops: be satisfied to strive for that.
- Do not underestimate the delight of real simplicity in your life style. Avoidance of affectation and unnecessary complications earns as much goodwill and love as pompous artificiality earns dislike.
- Try and keep your mind constantly on the pleasant aspects of life and on actions which can improve your situation. Try to forget everything that is irrevocably ugly or painful. This is perhaps the most efficient way of minimizing stress by voluntary diversion of your mind.
- Nothing paralyses your efficiency more than frustration: nothing helps it more than success. Even after the greatest defeats, thoughts of failure are best combated by taking stock of all your past achievements. There is always something, no matter how modest, in which we can take pride, and by so doing restore our self-confidence.
- When faced with a task which is very painful yet necessary, don't put it off: cut right into an

abscess to eliminate the pain, instead of prolonging it by gently rubbing the surface.
- Stress on one system helps relax another system: exercise reduces mental tension and anxiety.
- Work, but find an environment which is in line with your preferences and therefore eliminates the need for the frustrating constant readaptation which is the major cause of distress.

Selye refers to these ideas as useful tricks to minimize distress. They will be helpful to you as you analyse your lifestyle and maybe make changes in order to choose the arousal level most appropriate to you. If the demands and pressures you encounter are the ones you have chosen to face, they will be less distressful than those you face reluctantly. Also, if the stresses you accept and choose help you fulfill your ambitions, then their damaging effects will be minimal.

Bibliography

Arkle, W. A., *A Geography of Consciousness*. Neville Spearman, London, 1974.

Bandler, R. and Grinder, J., *Frogs into Princes*. Real Person Press, Moab, Utah, 1979.

Benson, H., *The Relaxation Response*. Fount Paperbacks, London, 1977.

Burns, D., *Feeling Good: the New Mood Therapy*. William Morrow & Co., New York, 1980.

Carruthers, M., *The Western Way of Death*. David-Poynter, London, 1974.

Coleman, V., *Stress Control*. Maurice Temple Smith, London, 1978.

Ellis, A. A. and Harper, R. A., *A Guide to Rational Living*. Institute for Rational Living, California, 1962.

Friedman, M. and Rosenman, R., *Type A Behaviour and Your Heart*. Greenwich, C. T., Fawcett, New York, 1974.

Gallwey, W. T., *The Inner Game of Tennis*. Random House, New York, 1974.

Gallwey, W. T., *Inner Tennis*. Random House, New York, 1976.

Heller, J., *Something Happened*. Knopf, New York, 1974.

Keyes, K., *Handbook to Higher Consciousness*. Fifth edition, Living Love Centre, California, 1975.

Little, B. *This Will Drive You Sane*. Compcare Publications, Minneapolis, 1971.

Melhuish, A., *Executive Health*. Business Books, London, 1978.

Prather, H., *I Touch the Earth, the Earth Touches Me*. Doubleday and Co., New York, 1972.

Seyle, H. *Stress Without Distress*. J. B. Lippincott, Philadelphia, 1974.

Smith, M. J., *When I Say No, I Feel Guilty*. Bantam, New York, 1975.

Stanton, H. E., *The Plus Factor: a Guide to Positive Living*. Fontana/Collins, Sydney, 1979.

Stanton, H. E., *The Healing Factor: a Guide to Positive Health*. Fontana/Collins, Sydney, 1981.

Sugerman, D. A. and Freeman, L., *The Search for Serenity*. Collier Macmillan, London, 1979.

Index

About the Author

After graduating from Melbourne University, Dr Stanton spent eight years teaching in secondary schools and five years lecturing in teacher training colleges. He has taught in the universities of South Australia and Tasmania since 1969, and is now Consultant on Higher Education at the University of Tasmania. He also runs a consultancy service for companies and the public sector, and has a private practice in clinical and sports psychology.

Dr Stanton is author of the following books, also published by Optima:

The Plus Factor: A Guide to Positive Living (February 1988)
The Healing Factor: A Guide to Positive Health (February 1988)
The Fantasy Factor: Using Your Imagination To Solve Everyday Problems (August 1988)